GO Write
And You Won't Go Wrong

WRITE YOUR BOOK IN 30 DAYS!

MICHAEL RAY KING

Go Write and You Won't Go Wrong: Write Your Book in 30 Days!

Copyright © 2012 by Michael Ray King
Copy Edit by Nancy Quatrano
Cover design and layout by Jonathan Pleska
Interior layout and pagination by Jeff Swesky

Michael Ray King
Go Write and You Won't Go Wrong: Write Your Book in 30 Days!
112. pgs
ISBN 978-1-935795-11-7 softcover
978-1-935795-12-4 Kindle
1. Education
2. Self Help Techniques
Library of Congress Control Number: 2012915386

All Rights Reserved. No part of this book may be reproduced, stored in a retrieval system, or transmitted in any form or by any means, electronic, mechanical, photocopying, recording, or otherwise, without permission in writing from MRK Publishing.

MRK Publishing
PO Box 353431
Palm Coast, FL 32135-3431
www.MichaelRayKingPublishing.com

Printed in the United States of America

Dedication Page

In writing books, many people come should appear on the dedication page. In writing *Go Write*, the list of folk I must mention is lengthy. I purposed to write this book to help others as I have been helped over the years. Without the eight days in West Virginia in the house I grew up in, handing out with my dearest Mother, this book may never have come to be. So, I dedicate this to my mother with all my heart for her support.

I also have a coach who helps me step into my dreams and aspirations. Without her help, I may never have stepped far enough outside my comfort zone to help others. So, I also dedicate this book to Janice Karm, an incredible coach and motivator who helps me see many possibilities.

My sister Nancy Williford, lifts me up when I'm down. This fact alone has me indebted to her. The same goes for the Rogues Gallery Writers, Nancy Quatrano, Bridget Callaghan, and Jeff Swesky. The four of us have forged a writers group of which to be proud. These people all support and encourage me each and every day.

My good friend Rik Feeney taught me much about how writing does not have to be a long and painful chore. I would be remiss not to acknowledge his encouragement and advice over the years.

Lastly, this book is dedicated to all the writers who need a hand up, a guide, a jumping off point, to get their book from an idea and into a real, tangible product. In other words, this is for everyone with a writing dream – this book is a means by which to deliver that dream into reality.

Table of Contents

A Brief Overview - **1**

Chapter One - **3**

   Pen, Pencil, Paper – the Three P's of Preparation
   Index Cards
   Comfortable Place to Write
   A "Sound" Acceptable Place to Write

Chapter Two - **8**

   Kill the Critic!
   Zip the Lip
   Schedule Writing Time the Day Before
   Scheduling Where to Write
   Use the Tools/Assistance Provided (don't go rogue)
   Do Not Revisit Material Already Written
   Post Word Count Daily and Use the Facebook Group

Chapter Three - **17**

   Select a Working Title that Reflects Overall Theme of Your Book
   Select a Subject to Write About for Which You Possess Passion and Knowledge
   Keep Your Title Focused on Niche Audience
   Working Title is not Written in Stone

Chapter Four - **20**

   Index Cards - One Chapter, One Card
   Write Short Phrases on Cards to Describe Chapter Content

Target 10 to 13 Chapters
Include Appendices as Separate Chapters
Author Bio
Setup an Index Card for Your Dedication Page

Chapter Five - **24**

Set up 4-6 Index Cards with Subtopic Items (one per card) to Flesh Out Chapter
Focus on Staying on Task
One Sentence/phrase - minor points
Think of Working Title While Writing
How to Use the Subtopic Cards

Chapter Six - **29**

Use of Technology - An Overview and the Dangers Involved
750words.com
Google Spreadsheet
Facebook Page
Thesaurus.com
Dictionary.com
Emails of Quotes with Tip of the Day Reference

Chapter Seven - **40**

The Coach
Time Constraints
Value of a Personal Coach

Appendix – Writing Encouragements - **44**

About the Author - **104**

Go Write and You Won't Go Wrong!
A Brief Overview

Hello. I appreciate your commitment to taking on the challenge of writing your book. This undertaking may have been in the works for years. Many people I work with desire to write a book but don't know how to begin. If they know how to begin, they find they cannot stay with the writing.

I designed this book to get you started and keep you rolling. From the simple instructions at the beginning to the daily encouragements in the appendix, Go Write and You Won't Go Wrong! keeps you writing to meet that goal – a finished first-draft manuscript.

This book is also a significant part of my webinar product by the same name. In the webinar, I coach you through the book writing process. Participants receive two daily emails to remind them to write. Each participant also receives a daily voice message designed to motivate and encourage.

Also included in the webinar is a Google Spreadsheet where the participants post their daily word counts. I also set up a Facebook Group page exclusively for participants in the webinar series. In addition, in three of the live webinars, I open up the phone lines for a Q & A session.

For those who wish to get to their book-writing goal in a more direct fashion, I also provide a weekly accountability phone call from myself. I designed this call to do a number of things. I want to find any stumbling blocks. I also desire to keep you motivated. One of my strengths is that I know how to keep people pumped up.

In a nutshell, here's the plan: You'll use index cards to set the book up. Then you'll determine what big idea or theme best describes your book. You'll select a working title, which we'll call "the head". Then we'll construct the skeleton, then the sinew, and finally, the ligaments.

By the time you complete these tasks, you'll be set to roll on through the writing. Be mindful of this: as long as you do as I ask, you'll complete your book on time. If you fall behind and don't catch up you won't complete your book in 30 days.

Okay, what if you complete your book in forty-five days? Is that so bad? Given that many people take years to write a completed manuscript, I believe that forty-five days is excellent, too.

Follow my instructions though, and let's get your book done in a month.

Let's get started!

Chapter One – Get Set Up

Pen, Pencil, Paper – The Three "P's" of Preparation

Since index cards supply an integral part of the *pre-writing* process in Go Write and You Won't Go Wrong!, a couple of simple decisions on your part as the writer, are needed. I believe you should always write from a certain level of comfort. For this reason, I like to start with simple decisions.

The three P's of preparation may seem a bit obvious, but I want you to think of the repercussions of how you construct your book's body. My three basic P's are Pen, Pencil, and Paper. These three P's only take a moment's thought, but there are benefits to starting out this way.

First, decide whether or not to write in pen or pencil. I recommend pencil because you may need to change some things. That said, most often I use pen because a) I prefer writing in pen, b) there is a permanency and confidence associated with writing in pen (for me), and c) I like to see the changes I've made on my cards. By striking through the changes with a single line rather than scratching them out (or erasing), I am able to go back and study the changes.

I realize index cards skirt the digital norm. Yes, index cards are very analog (non-digital), but I do this for a reason. Sometimes, it is better to have a tactile, spatial look at a project rather than a digital screen or everything on one piece of paper. In the case of writing a book, there are many good reasons to use index cards to build your book. I'll cover those in more detail as we go along.

The other P is Paper. Though I am a huge fan of technology, sometimes you just have to do things "old school" just for a little while. We'll get into some technology tools later on. I strongly suggest you follow my plan on writing your book. When you lay out the book in front of you, the index cards provide a view of your project that isn't as available with a notebook or a computer screen. I urge you to not skip over this method of using index cards to build the skeletal structure of your book.

Index Cards

As stated in the "Overview" chapter, your 'working title' will be the head, your chapters the skeleton, and your subtopics under each chapter your sinew – or the muscles and tendons of the book. Your writer's voice is the arterial network that pumps life into your words. Re-writing and editing will determine the outer skin, or the look of your book.

The index cards are provided as a tool to help you organize your book. Personally, I loathe outlines as they feel too formal and restrictive for my creativity. Many authors tout the use of index cards for this purpose as they allow them to "see" the book coming together.

Please do not discount the value you will find by using them. When setting up this book, I found plotting out

Go Write and You Won't Go Wrong

the index cards helped spur organizational ideas as well as creative ones and are designed to keep writers on task. The process of writing by hand brings you closer to your subject in a tactile manner. Trust me; this can be very beneficial to the process of writing.

Coming up in a couple of chapters, I'll explain how to use these index cards. Chapters 3 and 4 will give you step by step instructions. For now, just commit to using your cards. Remember - do as I suggest and you'll complete your book on time!

Comfortable Place to Write

Every writer knows a "special" place where they find it comfortable to write. For some, writing as they sit in a special chair works. Others may require a place with a view. Some people, like me, find it difficult to write at home with the many chores, honey-do lists, or children to distract us.

I enjoy writing at a quiet little restaurant or under a nice shade tree or even at the library. The restaurant is great because I can nibble on prepared food and not have to spend time preparing anything. The staff brings me whatever I need, and once you build a relationship with the waitress(es), familiarity can make the experience even more comfortable. I wrote my first book this way.

The library is great for me because simply walking in among the books fills me with a sense of comfortable urgency. I feel moved to create one of those wonderful, word-filled tomes that surround me. Most libraries give you free Wi-Fi and electrical outlets as well. This way I can use the tools of online *cloud computing* to augment my writing experience. The library can be a VERY comfortable and amenable place to write.

I've written at swimming pools, on bike trails, and on back decks of houses. Each writer has their own particular places they enjoy peace, tranquility, and the inspiration to move forward. I **strongly** suggest you allow yourself permission to find these places of comfort and use them.

A "Sound" Acceptable Place to Write

I purposefully avoided mentioning "noise" or "background sound" in the section above. Sound can be the most intrusive of distractions. One of the reasons I love writing in a restaurant is the "white noise" in the background. The clinking of dishes. The flow of customers. All this contributes to a comfortable background noise for me because I'm not responsible for any of the noises.

At home, I currently have four children in the house. They knock on my door even though I've admonished them to be quiet and try not to interrupt. Or they'll get into an argument and my parental ears perk up to determine the level of necessary involvement. Even friendly banter can distract me because I like to know what's happening in their lives.

Some writers solve noise issues with earphones and music. I enjoy listening to music when I write - sometimes. Most of the time, I prefer white noise and solitude. I've been known to take a vacation in the mountains for a week, by myself, simply to finish a

Go Write and You Won't Go Wrong

book. Pay close attention to your "comfort zone" and make sure the sound levels meet your desired input.

Lastly, consider your phone. I don't believe I've met an author yet that says, "Heck yeah! I love writing and taking phone calls!" I don't believe I ever will. For years, because of the nature of my business, I never went anywhere without my phone. Too many times I'd get interrupted by an "important" call. I believe strongly now that writers should turn their phones off when it's time to write.

Part of using the wonderful technology we now enjoy is the ability of our phones to take messages. Please do yourself a *huge* favor and do as I suggest - turn off your phone. Give yourself permission to write in your allotted time. For instance, I allowed myself three hours to write today. My phone is off and I'm going to exceed my word count dramatically. Sound can be our most invasive distraction. Don't allow noise to intrude on your special writing time, especially in your comfortable writing place. Defend that place with vigor.

Chapter Two – The Basics

Kill the Critic

The most difficult challenge most writers must overcome can be summed up with two words - The Critic. Even seasoned writers fight battles with their inner critic. When writing a first draft manuscript, the most imperative task for a writer, is to *kill the critic*.

Your inner critical voice or "judge" is the epitome of insidiousness. Check out the definitions of the word "insidious": 1 intended to entrap or beguile: an insidious plan. 2 stealthily treacherous or deceitful: an insidious enemy. 3 operating or proceeding in an inconspicuous or seemingly harmless way but actually with grave effect: an insidious disease.

The Critic, acts precisely in this manner. Some of the tactics the "judge" uses will be obvious. For instance, you may hear an inner voice that says, "Who are you to think someone will want to read your words?" Or, a more stealthy approach will be when The Critic whispers to your brain, "Just go back to that chapter you wrote yesterday and clean up some of that atrocious grammar."

Intellectually, you may *know* the chapter in question contains grammar issues. Your inner critic knows, too. A first draft is no place for a judge or critic. Grammar,

Go Write and You Won't Go Wrong

punctuation, continuity, and any other technical aspect of your writing will be handled in the editing phase. There is no place for mixing creation and editing. There is *no* editing on the first draft!

Creating a manuscript requires freedom. Freedom to write what you are passionate about. Freedom to experiment with your ideas and your perspective on the subject you write about. The instant you let The Critic through your mental "doors," creativity flees.

Beware of the subtleties of your inner critic. "Oh, just this *one* sentence. You could go back to yesterday's writing and do this so much better." Here's the big downside to giving in to The Critic during your first draft: once your critic finds something and fixes it, that critic wants more. The Critic feeds off your desire to produce a perfect manuscript.

"That's not a bad thing," you say. Of course it isn't, if we're discussing your final draft. But during your first draft, you'll end up inundated with correcting and perfecting a manuscript that has not yet been written. I cannot tell you how many writers I've met who remain stuck in this style of writing. They cannot fathom how a book could be written in 30 days. These writers cannot write a book in a year. Some will be working on the first chapter for the rest of their lives. And criticism kills creativity!

Please trust me on this. The scenario of writing without a critic proves much more productive and conducive to getting your words into a first draft manuscript. Write with unfettered passion and knowledge until you finish the task. Then employ tactical, efficient editing techniques that will polish your book, strengthen it, and get the book ready for publication far faster than struggling through the first draft with The Critic.

I found this out the hard way. I wrote poetry for twenty-eight years before I dared publish. Guess what? I immediately won three Royal Palm Literary Awards for my poetry in three successive years. In the twenty-eight years I allowed my judge to condemn me, I was convinced my writing should be sentenced to death, only good enough to be read by myself and a trusted few. Now, my poetry is read all over the world. I have poetry books selling in the UK.

So that's why I say, "Kill the critic." Sure, we'll resurrect this inner voice when the time is right. After all, an excellent critique can strengthen a good manuscript and make it great. Don't allow your judge to sentence your writing to life imprisonment. Keep the judge and critic out of your writing. Go for broke. Let it all spew out.

Zip the Lip

Being a poet, "zip the lip" best describes this mental tool. When writing a book, talking about the writing of it will steal your creativity one snippet at a time. When you don't preserve your ideas solely for the paper (or computer screen), your spoken words will dampen the zeal and passion you have for the project, over time.

Note I did not employ the word, might. Talking to others, non-writers in particular, about what you are writing *will* cause a "decay" in the creative passion for what you're writing. Not all at once, mind you. Over

Go Write and You Won't Go Wrong

time. There are appropriate times to speak about a writing project, but you must be diligent about determining how much you say and what you reveal.

This has nothing to do with the fear that someone might steal your work. Hogwash. I'm saying that your internal muse, your creative self, loses its passion for the writing if you expose it in words before you write it. And why open the door for your critic and judge to run screaming from their soundproof rubber rooms into the midst of your project?

It may be appropriate to talk about your book project at a trusted writers' group where you can get feedback and direction. A trusted writers' group feeds on creativity. These people understand what it takes to write. They understand your struggles. They can help you when you're stuck. Use a solid writers group respectfully, though. Be willing to give more to others than you ask to receive in the way of help. Writers groups are *most* valuable once you've finished your first draft. Try to use them during your initial writing only when absolutely necessary. That judge and critic would simply love to escape.

Schedule Writing Time the Day Before

Writers happen to be some of the most procrastination-oriented people on this planet. Given the choice to write or do nearly anything else, writing takes a back seat. Ask a writer what they love to do most? Write. Go figure.

This theme runs true for nearly every writer I meet. For this reason, and many, many more, I love Ray

Bradbury. The man wrote every day of his life from 1938 until his death in 2012, even after his stroke in 1999. This man *loved* to write. He lived to write.

One of the most common excuses I've heard (and given) over the past 13 years is the time factor. "I don't have time to write," many authors lament to me. I've even given voice to this in my day. Yet the truth is, if you have no more than a half-hour here and a half-hour there throughout your day, you can write a book in 30 days.

I am writing this book in eight days. The only reason the manuscript will take eight is that I am parceling out my time so that the work takes eight days. I'm on a working vacation in my home state of West Virginia. I want to keep my mind fresh and I want to meet up with old friends. I, therefore, *plan* when I'm going to write.

Staging out the writing time for my book is a practice I employ at home as well. My plans change often due to children, appointments, and phone calls, etc. By blocking out time, I ensure the writing will happen. Before you shut down for today, set up your blocks of time for tomorrow. Then, just follow the plan.

Scheduling Where to Write

Another tangent critical to scheduling your time to write is planning *where* to write. Most of us have busy, full lives and many commitments. In my case, a thing like school being out for the summer means I have to shift *where* I write.

Go Write and You Won't Go Wrong

While I love my children, and love being accessible to them, my writing gets stymied by constant interruptions. Whether the interruption is a knock at the door or I overhear issues going on within the house both are distractions and take me away from my writing.

Based on your circumstances, I urge you to *plan* where you will write. Using this planning technique as a tool to success, you will find yourself much more productive as well as much more inspired.

Use Tools/Assistance provided (don't go rogue…)

One of the key dangers every writer faces is the urge to go "rogue." For years I scoffed at the pundits and "successful" writers who told me to, "write every day." I told myself, "I am different. I can do this my way."

I struggled and sputtered and stumbled my way through three books. Then, when I committed to following the wisdom of those who've gone before me, I found that they understood key aspects of a writer's mentality and personality.

I'm providing you with all the tools you need to successfully produce a first draft manuscript in 30 days – a manuscript consisting of 30,000 words. This translates into around 120 to 150 pages in a book. When you follow my steps, use the tools like 750words.com, use the Google Spreadsheet, and when you commit to writing every day, you **will** succeed.

Trust me, when you go off on your own, too often you will reinvent the wheel and make things more difficult for yourself. Most new writers need guidance. That's what my full program is all about. I'll coach you through the process and get you to your book.

If you're taking advantage of the webinar, attend every single session. Get the most out of the tools and information I provide. I truly desire for you to succeed, to get that book out of your heart and into the world. Just like any birthing process, there are sacrifices to be made, disciplines to adhere to, and sometimes, pain.

In the end, everything you go through will be worth the effort when your book stares back at you from your screen, waiting for you to make it stronger, more intelligent, and presentable to the world. That work happens in the editing phase. Getting to the editing phase is what we're all about. I want to take you there. Please use the tools…

Do Not Revisit Material Already Written

I mentioned you should 'kill the critic' correct? Here is the door your judge and critic will storm through, even if you only open it a little. You may have to go back and read something you wrote to pick up the context or to see if you covered a subtopic completely, but you *must* guard against being critical of the words that came out of you.

Often as writers, we look back over our words and they seem foreign, like they didn't emanate from us. When we look over our first draft work, we often begin to fear our 'baby' is going to be ugly. Please trust me on this. We'll clean up our little one nicely in the edit and revision phase after the first draft is complete.

Go Write and You Won't Go Wrong

Remember, you can't edit blank pages, so unless you complete the first draft, there will **never** be a book!

Avoiding the debilitating pitfalls of the critic and judge requires vigilance and determination. I cannot warn you strongly enough to keep these voices at bay. They will add nothing to your manuscript and almost assuredly, they'll drag down your momentum.

Post Word Count Daily and Use the Facebook Group Page

The online Google Spreadsheet and Facebook Group Page are two tools you should employ to enrich your writing experience. In both places you'll find other writers attending your session of the webinar. Please use these tools to boost morale, both yours and that of the rest of the group as well.

When you post your word count, you get the satisfaction of making your efforts measurable. Here your progress is very black and white. This can be a very fulfilling and motivational exercise that validates your effort. By posting your word count, you also help motivate others who need to see other writers using the system.

You may draw motivation from seeing the other writers posting their word counts each day as well. I discovered this motivational perk in my focus writers group, the Rogues Gallery Writers. Whenever one of my fellow Rogues posted their daily word count to the other three, we each fed off the success. Positivity breeds positivity.

By posting your word count daily, you get a view of your progress. You'll be amazed at how much you get done on your book each day. If you happen to have a 'zero' day, post that as well. Others may easily be in the same boat and it's always good to know you're not the only one who misses a day every now and then. The goal is to write every day, but if life gets in the way, pick yourself up the next day and move forward.

The Facebook Group Page is a private, "by invitation only" group for attendees of my webinars and classes. My goal here is to create a community of writers who all wish to move forward in their writing and would like interaction with others taking on the same task. Interaction with other writers can help your writing in many ways.

One way is simply commiserating on some of the challenges of writing. Another may be encouraging someone who's struggling. Another may be someone helping you with ideas or encouragement. Camaraderie develops among writers who take the time to communicate with other writers. Try it out. You may be pleasantly surprised.

Chapter Three – Title and Subject

Working Title Should Reflect Theme of Your Book

When coming up with a working title for your book, you want the title to tell your potential audience exactly what the book is about. This book is titled "Go Write and You Won't Go Wrong! Write Your Book in 30 Days!" My desired message is to tell potential readers that writing **everyday** will get you to a book in 30 days.

Yes, the "writing every day" aspect is insinuated, not stated in the title, but you also want something catchy that will allow potential readers to 1) remember your book and 2) be able to Google your book's domain. In every venue, I'll be pounding home the importance of writing every single day. I'll also reinforce the **fact**, that when you follow my suggested path, you will possess a first draft manuscript in 30 days.

Focus on a title that delivers the flavor, the importance, and the gist of your book. Don't panic, your title does not have to be perfect from the outset. This is simply the 'working title'. More on that in a moment.

Select a Subject to Write about for Which You Possess Passion and Knowledge

In the early development stages of coming up with your working title, keep focused on what you desire the book to be about. Writers, especially new writers, often want to write everything in their first book. By using the title as a focal point, you can keep from chasing after shiny object distractions that lead to a convoluted book. Focus your working title on a niche topic that you're passionate to share, and then determine each step of the way if what you plan to put in your book falls into that niche. If not, save the idea for a subsequent book. Look at your working title as a type of "mission statement." Who is your audience and what is your book going to solve for them? These questions will get you on the path to the title that will keep you focused on *your* mission.

Trust there will be tangents you desire to follow when writing your book. Use your title to stay on track. Your passion and knowledge will help lead you to a great working title. Allow your passion and knowledge to suggest more than one title if need be. Play with them. Run them over in your head. Combine them, mold them, and see what you come up with. Use your passion and knowledge to your best advantage.

Keep Your Title Focused on Niche Audience

Writing for "everyone" will never work. You should have a niche or targeted audience who would be interested in your book's subject matter. Broad audiences, such as "all men" or "all women" are a recipe for the death of a book. Target your working title to appeal to that select group of people to which you will be writing.

The passion and knowledge referenced above will help tremendously, but it's easy to get carried away and want to appeal to the whole world. If you really want your book to be read, focus your title to appeal to your target audience. Use keywords (which can be phrases) that will catch the eye of someone in that audience. By keeping the niche audience in mind with your title, you also help your writer's voice stay focused on the task at hand.

You cannot be everything to everyone. The writer who realizes this, writes a book that speaks directly to their targeted niche audience, grabs them with a title they understand, and therefore increases the prospects of their book becoming successful.

Working Title Not Written in Stone

Remember, your working title simply exists to guide you along the writing path. As you write your book, most likely you will come up with tweaks and changes to your title. You may realize you want to throw out the original working title altogether. Feel free to play with it over the course of writing your book.

That stated, when you get the title you want, and you know it, *really* know it, go to the Internet and buy the domain name. The title to this book was changed a couple of times simply because someone else already owned the domain name that corresponded to my title. In the end, I preferred the final title over the original, mainly because the original wasn't so original. Otherwise the domain would have been available, correct?

Chapter 4 – Set Up Chapters (Build the Skeleton)

Index Cards - One Chapter, One Card

We'll now build our book's skeleton. You've chosen the subject on which you're going to write. You have passion for this subject and you possess knowledge about it. Here is where you prove this. On a piece of paper or your computer, write out all the different aspects your book will need to address in order to cover your subject. We'll break these aspects into chapters. When you write your chapter names, write them in simple phrases.

For instance, for this book I listed my chapters as 1) Preparation and Setup 2) Working Title/Subject 3) Setting Up Chapters 4) Sinewing Out the Chapters 5) Tools 6) Writing Tips 7) Using the Cloud 8) Encouragements. Each chapter, once I wrote down the words or phrases, got its own index card.

Take out your index cards. Once you have some chapters written down, transfer the chapter phrases to their own card. Write the word Chapter in the upper left hand corner. Write the 'working chapter number' beside it. You may rearrange your chapters later. This is one of the reasons I suggested you may wish to use pencil. Again, I like pen because I can track where the chapters have moved during the course of the writing (if at all).

Go Write and You Won't Go Wrong

Once you've written the word "Chapter" and "1", then write the word or phrase for that chapter in large letters on the face of the index card. Once you complete this, get another card and write "Chapter" and "2" on it. Repeat with the word or phrase on the face of the second card. Continue this until you exhaust your chapter titles.

Write Short Phrases on Cards to Describe Chapter Content

The chapter titles should be short phrases or words that embody the overall information you wish to deliver in the chapter. We will be breaking the chapter down into subtopics that flesh out the chapters soon. For now, make sure the chapter is a logical, overarching step toward the total theme of your book. Your chapter should carry your book forward in a giant step. Make sure your chapters are not giant leaps. We desire to take the reader on a journey, and each chapter should move forward by a very significant "step."

The short phrases or single words should be highly descriptive of the chapter. Many times, using keywords that relate strongly to your subject matter works well here. Avoid using sentences and paragraphs because that will infringe drastically on our next step which comes in the next chapter.

Target 10 to 13 Chapters

Don't panic. For the purposes of completing your book in 30 days, I am suggesting this number of chapters to facilitate a 'numbers view' of what we're doing. You may adjust this number to whatever number of chapters you need. This book "*Go Write and You Won't Go Wrong!*" only has 9 chapters. Your chapter count will be determined by how many you need to complete your book.

In order to write a book in 30 days, there will be a daily word/subtopic count you will need to attain each day. The more chapters you have, the more subtopics you will have. The more subtopics you have, the more word count required each day. I like to suggest writers go for 10 chapters with no more than six subtopics per chapter.

This means the writer will be writing 60 subtopics. Writing two subtopics a day at 500 words per subtopic will complete your book in 30 days at approximately 30,000 words which would come out to be anywhere from 100 pages to 150 pages depending on what size book you choose. So stick with 10 to 13 chapters. If you need more chapters, adjust accordingly.

Include Appendices as Separate Chapters

If your book will require an appendix or appendices, make out a separate index card for each appendix just like a chapter. Instead of writing "Chapter" in the upper left corner of the card, write "Appendix" followed by A if there will be more than one. If only one, simply "Appendix" will do. The second appendix would get its own card and be labeled "Appendix B"

Many books do not require an appendix. Don't try to force one if an appendix is not needed. Also, if a Glossary of terms is needed due to particularly specialized language in the book, I highly recommend you set up a separate index card for your glossary.

Author Bio

You need to have a separate index card for your author bio. Label this index card "Author Bio" in the upper left hand corner. To keep uniformity throughout this process, having a separate card for each of these book aspects will help keep you on track. The goal is to get you through the first draft writing of your book in 30 days. The author bio is not necessary in the first draft, but I believe having this information in front of you keeps you focused on the completion of your book.

Bios can be difficult to write for first time authors. So, by writing your bio as a first draft inclusion to the book, you allow for more editing and fine tuning of your bio. No sense putting off something you will need as part of your book later when you can complete it now.

Setup an Index Card for Your Dedication Page

There will be many people you wish to thank on your dedication page. Or, maybe you'll only have one. This is a very individual page. In order to not forget or have someone special fall through the cracks, keep this card handy for whenever a person helps you in a manner that deserves inclusion in the dedication. Again, this may be one person but could be many. You don't want to get to publication and remember you forgot to add so-and-so to the dedication.

Chapter 5 – Sinewing Out the Chapters

Set up 4-6 Index Cards with Subtopic Items (one per card) to Flesh out Chapter

Lay out all your chapter cards. Pick a chapter and think of items or 'subtopics' that would flesh out your chapter. Write down a phrase or sentence that describes this subtopic on an index card. Repeat this process until you have four to six subtopic cards for each chapter. When thinking of these subtopics, consider the steps or logical progressions needed to flesh out your chapter completely.

You know your subject. You know what it will take to complete your chapter. You know the information needed to take the chapter from start to finish. These four to six cards will be the writing prompts you will use to write the body of your book. Make your sentence or phrase very descriptive. Don't worry about grammar. The sole purpose of these cards is to prompt you on what to write to fill in the necessary information that will make your chapter work.

For fiction writers, pick out key elements you wish to use in each chapter. You may not be a writer who can come up with all your chapters in the beginning. Even nonfiction writers add chapters as they write. Fill out all the chapters and sub topics you can. Then, as your book unfolds, make sure you write cards for each chapter you add and each subtopic you come up with.

The goal is to be able to place all your index cards out on a table and get a bird's eye view of your book. A book is a living, breathing creation, so don't feel you have to come up with all or even most of your index cards in the beginning. You do, of course, need to come up with some.

Focus on Staying on Task

There will be a temptation to over-write your chapters. Work hard to group your thoughts into sections that will deliver all the information you need to cover your chapter. I realize I'm repeating this thought quite a bit, but I cannot stress the importance of these subtopics enough. When you write subtopics that take the reader off on tangents, you only make your book less readable. You desire to write the best book possible. Stay away from tangents.

Focus on your chapter and make sure your subtopic cards reflect your chapter's critical information. As mentioned before, these cards possess the important aspect of being the prompts from which you will write the body of your book. More on that in a moment. First, a couple of tips for maximizing the use of your subtopic index cards.

One Sentence/phrase - minor points

When you limit your subtopic to one sentence or a phrase, there will be plenty of room on your card to write down additional ideas. These ideas should be one or two words that relate directly to your subtopic. These words will help prompt you on items you feel must be included in the chapter. This tip becomes huge when you write how-to books or self-help books where there can be a lot of steps or ideas you wish to present in each subtopic. Remember, these cards are tools to help you remember the ideas you wish to present most in your book.

Think of Working Title While Writing

Earlier, I described this process in terms of a human body, with the title being the head, the chapters the skeleton, and the subtopics the muscles and tendons. Your writer's voice will supply the lifeblood of energy, and editing is like the shaping of the skin. To get your book to its strongest possible position, work your subtopics with the overall view of the book—the title—in mind.

How does your subtopic relate to the chapter title and how does it align with the overall focus of your book. The meat of your book, the bulk of your writing, will take place in conjunction with these subtopic cards. The better you align your subtopics with your chapters and the overall theme of your book, the stronger the first draft you'll have to work with during the editing process. Keeping that focus will also help you think of other subtopics as well as other potential chapters.

How to Use the Subtopic Cards

Once you have your subtopic index cards written for each chapter, label them in the upper right hand corner of the card with letters, A, B, C, and so forth, in the order you wish to present the subtopics in the chapter. Remember, these cards are only a guide. Once you get writing, if you believe subtopic "C" should be subtopic "E", make the change.

Mark any changes on your card whenever you make that decision. As I stated earlier, I use a pen and just strike-through the old letter with one line and write the new letter to the **left** of the old. The card set up is deliberate: "Chapter" is on the far left and "Subtopic" is on the far right to make sure there would be enough room if you moved subtopics and chapters around a lot.

Most of my chapters stay the same, although writing this book, the Chapter 6 that I started out with on the cards became "Chapter 2." Sometimes you don't see the complete layout of a book until you begin writing. I noted that the information in the original Chapter 6 was far too vital to keep where I slated it to go. So I moved it up. The card style allows you to do this easily.

Subtopics will move around a lot more. In order to complete a chapter, the flow sometimes needs to change from your first knee-jerk position. Nothing wrong with this at all. Do not be surprised if things move around a bit in the editing stage as well. Once you get 'other' eyes on the manuscript, you may find their input brings to light valuable information that causes some movement within the manuscript.

Once you've laid out all your chapters with subtopic index cards, you are now ready to write your book. Make sure you review Chapter Two in order to get your mindset right. Keep your focus clear of the critic, distractions, and the urge to revise text already written. This is your first draft. Plenty of time for revision later.

When you sit down to write, you should have set aside time, selected a comfortable, writer-friendly space, and secured a noise-level area that suits your personal requirements for good concentration. Go through your subtopic cards and select the ones that strike your passion most. One way to do this is to lay them all out on a flat surface in columns underneath the chapter cards. This gives you a bird's eye view of your book.

Avoid writing your book from chapter one through the rest of the chapters unless you feel strongly passionate about what you're writing. Remember your writer's voice? Here's where that lifeblood of your book shows through.

Fiction Writing Tips

Fiction writers should really pay attention to not writing linearly. By writing different subtopic cards from various portions of your book, you can keep the writing from being predictable.

Some of my fiction writers have used their cards as a living outline. By this I mean that they write up the cards they can, and as ideas come to them from their writing, they create more cards. Often fiction writers don't have nor desire everything to be planned out.

Other fiction writers I've spoken with have told me they love the "mindmapping" method. They use mindmapping to create their cards as they go. The important thing is to find a structural system that works for you. One that allows you to get your book finished in a reasonable amount of time.

Chapter 6 – Tools

Use of Technology - An Overview and the Dangers Involved

In this chapter I will introduce you to a number of basic, free Internet technologies that can offer a huge boon to your writing. My goal is to conduct my webinars with as much interaction and accountability as possible without the technologies becoming oppressive or stifling. Most writers I meet, both as a fellow writer and as a publisher, struggle to write, by their estimation, because of a lack of time.

I listen empathetically, but I've lived the truth. The truth is that any writer can find an hour of time to write, every day. Most writers I know struggle in the realm of time management. The technologies and sites I suggest below offer potent motivational and accountability aspects. They're easy to understand and are easily accessible.

I must forewarn though, of what I call IDS - Internet Distraction Syndrome. IDS eats away at our lives every day. Email, Facebook, Pinterest, Yahoo News, and literally thousands of other programs whittle away at the time we should spend on productivity. One innocent peek into Facebook can translate into a half hour of lost time for me. The same with Yahoo News. I love to keep up with sports and global news.

Email still haunts me as a time-waster. I do not suggest here that emails should not be answered. I simply suggest you schedule a time and place in your day to accomplish this feat. Time blocking has been proven to be one of the most successful time management tools. If you don't use it, by the time you clear away all the distractions, your motivation to write usually feels diminished or is gone entirely. Creativity should be tapped when your energies register high on your internal monitor. Distractions debilitate creativity.

Beware of IDS - Internet Distraction Syndrome. Keep your focus on your writing. Reward yourself for writing 2000 words with a 30-minute assault on all the online distractions you love. Hold your "dessert" until after the main course - your writing. In the long run, your book will be stronger and be completed faster than it would if IDS gets in the way.

A slight reverse of the previous paragraph can work as well. At times I find it beneficial to reward myself with a writing project. I love blogging and writing so much I often need to take care of business before I write. I then look at my writing as a "dessert" to savor. One of the keys in this scenario is to make sure you leave yourself time to write. That includes time to get to your "special" writing location.

750words.com

The site **750words.com** motivates writers. The site offers some really cool motivational aspects and they offer them at minimal charge. 750words.com does solicit (very passively in my estimation) donations if you like what they offer. I love what they offer and I've donated a few bucks to them. Allow me to run through some of the key benefits of the site that can definitely help you as a writer. All the aspects of the site helped me at one time or another.

When you create your account with 750words.com (free), you have the wonderful option of receiving an email prompt reminding you to write your 750 words today. You may set the time for when your email will arrive in your inbox. You do this in the "Settings" tab at the top of the page. I set my email delivery for 7:00am each day. If I haven't written my 750 words by the afternoon, "Buster" (750words) sends me another email reminding me to write. I love this. The emails are not obtrusive, but an effective reminder nonetheless.

When I write **before** my scheduled email reminder arrives, Buster sends me a nice note telling me I've already written my words for the day and to relax and enjoy my day. They even send a picture of a rose. I thought that was pretty cool.

Login: I love the ability to log in to sites from my Facebook account. I don't have to remember another password. I don't have to wonder if I'll be going through the "forgot password'" routine yet again. I simply click "login through Facebook" and I'm on my way. Yes, you may login with a password or Twitter or some other login, but I like Facebook. To each his own.

Once you login, I recommend you proceed straight to your writing. I've tweaked my setting with regard to my background screen color when I'm keying. I found I don't like the standard white. Last year, I went with a soft purple, almost lavender, and love it.

When you're keying your words, take note of the lower right hand corner where there is a running word count. There are two lines there: the "saved" line and the underlined and bolded word count. The system automatically saves what you write each minute. If you try to leave the screen before the minute is up, you will get a warning message asking if you wish to leave. Simply wait without keying anything, until the minute passes, and your writing will be saved.

750words.com offers a lot of cool aspects to these 'saved' writings. You may go back as far as you like and revisit your writing from past days, months, and years. Across the top of your screen stands a series of boxes, one for each day of the month. When you complete your 750 words, an "X" is placed in the box, like you would score a 'strike' in bowling. If you write less than 750 words, you will see a slash "/" in the box like you would score a spare in bowling. Of course, if you write nothing at all, your box remains empty.

For the purposes of writing your book, you may write here with complete privacy. You may opt to make your 750words account public, but most writers do not wish their first draft work to be seen publicly. I agree with that.

Since 750words is a word processing program, you may copy and paste your writing into Microsoft Word when you're done. Since your writing is stored here in perpetuity, you may opt to copy and paste into Word once a month or when you're done with your draft. I recommend you copy and paste daily, placing your work on your computer and a backup thumb drive. I've had too many computer crashes in my day to lose material through some crazy glitch. I've used 750words.com for over two years now, and I have had no problems with the site. But just in case...

In addition to archiving your work for you, 750words.com offers some cool feedback on your writing. The program actually analyzes your words and gives you feedback on your mood, your most-used words, your focus on past, present, or future, your topics of concern whether they be money, family, death, etc. These analytics can be massively handy.

Let's say you desire a certain piece of writing to come across with a specific mood in mind. Write what you feel will set that mood, then check the mood analytics. I've done this and the feedback was amazing. I also like the rating system as to word usage, especially adult word usage. You get rated just like the movies. Sometimes I check my rating and I'm at an "R" rating when I don't want to be so graphic. I can then go back and tone it down a bit.

One of the little fun things this site offers is the Monthly Challenge. The challenge is simple - write 750 words every single day of the month. Each month I've noted around 800 people take on the challenge. Only around 37% ever complete the challenge. This is my fifth consecutive month entering and it will be my third completion of the challenge. That's a 60% completion rate. I love being ahead of the norm.

What do you get when you successfully complete the challenge? The reward from 750words.com is a listing of your name on the Wall of Awesomeness with the other writers who successfully completed the challenge.

If you do not successfully complete the challenge, your name is placed on the Wall of Shame with the other writers who did not complete their task. It's all in fun.

The other reward you receive is self-delivered. When you sign up for the challenge, you have to key in what you will reward yourself with for completing the challenge. You also must list what penalty you'll pay if you don't. Many of us pay 750words.com a nominal amount of money like $5 when we don't complete the challenge. This helps keep the site up and running and gives us a financial stake, albeit a small one. Again, this is all in fun. Many months I write that if I do not complete my challenge, I will do a particularly difficult chore around the house I've been putting off. That can be a *huge* motivator to write!!

There are a number of other aspects of this site available to you as well. The ones I listed are the ones I use and enjoy. They add some fun to the writing and I look forward to logging in each day. One thing I did not mention. With regard to word count, you don't have to scroll down to the bottom of the page to get your daily count. Just glide your cursor over the boxes at the top and your word count will be displayed. This comes in handy for the next Internet tool.

Google Spreadsheet

For my webinars, I set up a Google Spreadsheet with columns for each writer taking the course. Typically, this spreadsheet contains 12 columns, one for the date, one for each writer and one for me. I then privately share the spreadsheet with each participant. Each day, participants are to log their word count for the day. I encourage not only including the word count for their book, but any word count from blogs or other writing projects as well.

The purpose of this spreadsheet is to motivate not only the writer logging their count, but the other writers as well. I learned in my focus writers group that I got motivated when my fellow writers posted their accomplishments. Also, I created a Facebook Group chat room for writers to discuss their projects with other writers. This is a private group with no outside 'non-writers' invited. This Facebook Group Page is for writers only.

Another purpose of logging your word count to the daily spreadsheet is accountability. I stress I do not wish the spreadsheet to be used as a negative tool. Life happens. I committed at the beginning of this year to write every single day. I'm halfway through the year and there are seven empty boxes on my 750words.com account. Those empty boxes are not failures but learning experiences. I now know when I go off for multi-day conferences to meticulously plan when and where I will write. I identify where my Wi-Fi hotspot is in advance and I stick to the plan. I lost three of the seven days to this issue alone.

By taking an active role and posting your words for others to see each day, you build in some accountability. This also allows me to see who is rocking along and more importantly, who I can step in and possibly help. The goal is to get your book done in a timely manner. My main mission here is to see that you do it.

When a writer posts a zero on the page, this can be motivational as well. Other writers may be feeling self-conscious about not writing one day. To see a fellow writer post the zero shows others that the world does not end and the writing continues. I have one participant at this time that will miss a day or two each week. But she's back posting her count again and has remained in high spirits through the whole process.

If you do not take the webinar, I still strongly recommend you use the Google Spreadsheet tool. This places your word count on the computing "cloud" so you may access the information from any computer or smart phone regardless of where you may be. I keep my webinar word count on a Google Spreadsheet and my personal monthly word count on a separate spreadsheet.

My personal monthly word count is particularly motivational. I strive to hit a minimum of 35,000 words per month. As I move forward, my goal is to get to where I write 50,000 words per month. When you look at the numbers, 50,000 words per month are only 1667 words a day, for a 30 day month. That translates into a little over 3 pages per day. I literally could write that many words each day in one hour.

Use this tool. It's a great way to pump yourself up as well as others who strive to accomplish the same goal as you - completion of a book.

Facebook Page

In order to create dialogue between present and past attendees of the webinar, I created a private Facebook page where participants may speak freely about their writing experience and share their struggles and triumphs. This is something I strongly encourage. My belief is that we need to adopt an atmosphere of helping each other rather than one of pure competition.

As our world shrinks more and more through increased communication and population, the need for cooperation will increase dramatically. Writers are the perfect group of people to promote this idea. By sharing in the experience of writing a book, not only does everyone gain motivation and commiseration, one of the side effects could be a more cooperative, less competitive world.

I'm not knocking competition, but save that for areas of life where it flourishes and is needed. The writing industry is crying out for help these days. Authors have lost their way as the greed and mismanagement of long-standing publishers collapses. Forging a new, brighter future for writers is within our grasp if we will only pluck it from the weeds of greed.

I truly desire the Facebook page to be highly interactive. I include past graduates of the webinar so they might add their experiences and ideas to the mix. The goal is to create a community of writers who *know* how to get it done!

Thesaurus.com

This tool stands as a bit dangerous for me to suggest. The tendency to step toward the critic and judge here concerns me. Thesaurus.com embodies an excellent tool to help you find the exact word you want. 99.9% of the time, you should simply write through your first-draft manuscript, selecting the closest word you can bring to mind. There come those rare moments, however, when only one special word works, and the rest of what you write depends on identifying that singular word.

In this case **only**, use the free thesaurus online. Once you move to the editing phase, make thesaurus.com your best friend. Use this tool, **when in edit**, to chase down better, stronger words than your first draft musters. For now, please, use this tool *very* sparingly. In fact, I may be foolish for even mentioning it. Yet, there is that .01% of the time during a first draft when the thesaurus becomes critical...

Dictionary.com

Like with the thesaurus, it's possible to get bogged down with this tool. With spell check available, why would I even suggest this tool? Sometimes two words sound exactly alike, but have entirely different meanings. To find the correct meaning, you will need a dictionary. One of my most vexing examples of this is "imminent" vs "eminent." If you guess wrong, this mistake may never be caught by editors, unfortunately. The words are not spelled incorrectly, but many people, even editors, do not know the difference. Another majorly misused couple of words are antidote and anecdote. The crazy thing with these two words is they truly are not even homonyms (words that sound exactly the same).

Do not use the dictionary for anything other than in this instance. Allow the spell checker to take care of most of your spelling issues. Most issues with words like *there, their*, and *they're*, editors hone in on easily. Keep that critic locked up, trust your editing process, but if you have a word like the one I listed above, take a moment to select the right one.

Emails of Quotes with Tip of the Day Reference

Over the course of the webinar, each and every day I send out an email with a quote from a famous writer. I do this for a number of reasons. One reason stems from the fact that I do not want 750words.com to be the only accountability you have to write each day. Sometimes a quote about writing from a famous author inspires a writer to forge ahead. I know these quotes help me. I can resonate with the observations made by these people who preceded me in the writing arena.

Another reason for the quotes and encouragement stems from the fact that every writer I ever met needs encouragement. In the appendix of this book you will find daily encouragement. In my first webinar I sent these quotes via email. I found participants enjoyed the motivational writing so much they dug into their emails to copy and paste them into a folder on their computer. While writing this book, I decided I should give the webinar participants all the quotes so they don't have to work so hard to find them.

Each day I will encourage you to read the tip of the day and take it to heart. Yes, nothing stops you from reading through them all right now. In fact, I encourage you do just that. I also encourage you to revisit these texts every day when I send out the quote. My goal is to motivate you to write every day. I use 750words.com to help me achieve this. I use posting on the Google Spreadsheet to achieve this. I use the private Facebook page to achieve this. I use my emailed quotes to achieve this. I read the writing tip of the day to achieve this.

Chapter 7 – Accountability Coach

The Coach

The piece de resistance regarding motivation to be successful in this quest, each participant in the webinar will receive a 10-15 minute accountability call from a professional transformational coach. This call will be designed to find out where you are in the process of writing your book, identify any snags you may run into, and to encourage and support your effort.

Janice Karm currently works as my personal coach. She defines positivity and possibilities. Janice is known as Ms. Possibilities. Her business name, Possibilities Unlimited, truly defines her approach. Each of us needs a positive force in our lives to help move us forward, especially when we take on a project larger than our comfort zone.

Adding Janice as the accountability coach for participants in the webinar stands as one of the most beneficial aspects of the entire program. When you receive your personal one-on-one call, you'll be fired up to keep writing! That goal defines the entire thrust of the "Go Write and You Won't Go Wrong!" program.

Time Constraints

I mentioned two critical points above. One is that the accountability call each week will last for 10 to 15 minutes. Janice will have a list of vital questions to ask you to make sure you remain on track. The number one reason people do not succeed in this course is they get off track. Janice's job is to keep you on track or help get you back on track. Since we run two classes a week, this means Janice follows up on twenty writers each week. Please respect the time allotted. Be prepared for your call with any questions or concerns to get the most out of your call.

The other item mentioned above is that Janice is my personal coach. She has been overwhelmingly positive and largely responsible for helping me turn my chaotic life into a more focused, productive, relaxed life. You may wish to inquire about her services. Coaching is her business and I would go so far as to say coaching is her calling.

If you keep getting stuck on moving forward in your life, whether the issue is business, writing, personal, or any other area, I would encourage you to look into a personal coach. While your accountability call is not the time to get that information, you may, and I encourage you to, ask her for an appointment to find out more about her coaching. Feel free to mention your interest on your call. She will set up a time to talk more at a later scheduled time. I want your accountability call to be positive, effective, and motivational.

Value of a Personal Coach

I actually have two coaches. In this last section I simply desire to impress upon you that most very successful people employ coaches. I go to conferences and meet famous people who, one would think, no longer need a coach. I'm told at every turn that a personal coach is invaluable.

My experience thus far with personal coaching is this: without Janice and Rothar (my other coach), I would still be languishing in a black pool of negativity stirred by my self-limiting beliefs and lack of confidence. Read or listen to any of the great pundits and people of knowledge and they all say that, without a coach to help them see where they limit themselves, they would not be able to achieve what they have.

A great coach is as valuable as a great editor. My transition from "stuck in my own little box" to "stepping out and helping others" can be directly linked to my pursuit of positive people interested in my development. I still have a long trek ahead of me. Instead of looking at that trek as fraught with trouble, roadblocks, and frustration, I now look forward to moving ahead with excitement.

Once I understood I could help people with what I know, everything changed. I no longer struggle with a job; I now possess a mission to help people achieve their writing goals. This major step forward came about through personal coaching. Yes, I must still do the tasks involved, but my entire outlook shifted from constant roadblocks to unlimited possibilities. See? I told you Janice's business name was appropriate.

If you're stuck, consider getting unstuck. Not just unstuck, consider you could achieve your heart's desire. Invest in yourself. Hire a great personal coach. For the record, I do not benefit from any coaching contract you may sign with Janice. I pay her for her outstanding professionalism and knowledge on how to be the best accountability coach ever. If you should choose to contract with her for coaching services, I applaud you. If you don't, that's fine as well.

"Go Write and You Won't Go Wrong!" ~

Michael Ray King

Appendix

This appendix contains daily writing tips and encouragements to help you along your way while writing your book. Each day, you will receive an email that contains a writing quote as well as the suggestion you turn the pages in this book to a particular Writing Encouragement.

Please make full use of this feature. One of the most critical aspects of writing a book is to stay motivated. These encouragements or "tips" were written with you in mind. Using all the tools available will help keep you on track.

Go Write and You Won't Go Wrong

Writing Tip #1

Mindmapping and Freewriting

Today is your first "Writing Tip" day. My goal here is to provide you with the tools needed to achieve the goal of completing a first draft manuscript in 30 days. Getting started tends to overwhelm many new writers. The scope of their book looms so large that creativity is nearly stifled. I'm here to assure you that the "Go Write and You Won't Go Wrong!" system hands you the tools necessary to break down the process of writing a book into very manageable steps.

Two effective tools with which to begin are mindmapping, and freewriting. In the main text of this book, I gave you a system using index cards. I realize setting up your cards may cause you some level of struggle. Employing a mindmap can help you get on your way.

Take a sheet of paper, turn it landscape rather than portrait, and draw a circle in the middle of the paper. In the circle write the main topic of your book using only a couple of words. Then, think of things that need to be written to flesh out the book. For each idea, draw a line to another circle and write a couple of words in the circle to denote that idea. Repeat this with as many supporting points of the book as you can.

Sometimes, an idea for a chapter will pop into your head, and then ideas to support that chapter come as well. Once you draw the line to the chapter circle, draw lines off the chapter circle for the things you know must fill that chapter.

Do you see where this connects with the index cards? Each chapter will become an index card. Each supporting point, what I call "subtopics" in every chapter, will become an index card. The mindmapping technique is a tried and true method to personally 'think tank' an idea or concept. If you get stuck coming up with your chapters and subtopics, this will help.

Once you get your subtopics identified, there may come a time when you feel you cannot write. This situation begs for freewriting. One of the simplest cures for writer's block comes in the form of freewriting. The process is quite easy to understand.

Begin writing whatever thoughts roll across your brain. If you're thinking, "I don't know what to write," those words become precisely *what* you write. If you keep thinking those words over and over again, you write them over and over again. You do not stop writing for ANYTHING. Do not stop to think, do not stop to look out the window, do not stop to rest. You write stream-of-consciousness—whatever comes to mind.

I recommend that while you do this, you make sure your cards sit on your table or desk beside you, spread out so you can see them. I also suggest that you read them over before you sit down to write. As you write your stream-of-consciousness writing, something in those cards will eventually pull your mind in that direction. Once you slide into the subtopic, keep writing.

You may find quite a bit of amazement in the "writing-release" mechanism freewriting gives you. I've found freewriting useful and enjoyable over the years. When you place this tip into your arsenal of tools, it will help make your writing experience easier and more fun, so

"Go Write and You Won't Go Wrong!"
~ Michael Ray King

Writing Tip #2

Writing Zone

Most writers have personal preferences concerning where and how to write. There truly is no right or wrong way to identify these things. Some prefer absolute privacy and silence, while others prefer music and white noise. I've found I enjoy writing at the library and in restaurants. I also enjoy writing on my iPhone while riding my bicycle and listening to jazz, but let me point out that I ride where there is very little traffic. In fact, due to concern over me possibly wrecking, I've gone to pulling off the bike path and then keying my thoughts

Ok, so that last example is a bit dangerous, but I literally have written some pretty good stuff that way. Let me encourage you to find that "comfort zone" that best fits you. Also, remember—no judgments on the first draft. Just let it flow. Don't be concerned about grammar and punctuation. Simply allow your story to come out.

"Go Write and You Won't Go Wrong!"
~ Michael Ray King

Go Write and You Won't Go Wrong

Writing Tip #3

Short Sentences

Today's reader doesn't like long sentences. Everyone wants things quick and easy. I'm going to suggest something of a writing mechanism you may at least wish to think about when you're writing. When you get to a point where you want the reader to get excited, make your sentences **very** short. Then, when you want to slow down the action or emotion a bit, write a longer sentence.

While this may be done during the editing process, keeping this in mind when you write your first draft can help you amp up your *own* excitement. This is a small 'trick of the trade' tip, but it's a tip worth remembering.

Remember, keep your sentences short unless you want to slow down the pace. Conjunctions like "and" and "but" should be eliminated as often as possible to help the reader.

"Go Write and You Won't Go Wrong!"
~ Michael Ray King

Writing Tip #4

Missed Day

My goal this year was to write every single day of the year. So far, I've missed five. When you slip up and miss a day, don't allow that to get you down. In the overall scheme of things, missing a day here and there does not mean you will not complete your book. This year, I'm writing an average of over 30,000 words a month. Getting into the habit of missing days will place you solidly back into old patterns, though.

When you hit 1000 words and you're on a roll, don't stop! Keep writing while the passion is hot. There are times I write 3000, 4000, even 5000 words in a day simply because I allow excitement and passion for what I'm writing to run loose. You can do this. If you're feeling it and you've hit that 1000 word mark, let 'r rip!

Keep going!

"Go Write and You Won't Go Wrong!"
~ Michael Ray King

Go Write and You Won't Go Wrong
Writing Tip #5

2P, 2F

Success in writing is about four things: *permission, passion, fortitude*, and *forgiveness*. No one I've ever met that desires to write a book lacked passion for their subject. Talk to almost anyone and they will tell you they've considered writing a book. Why do some people complete the task while others take their stories to the grave?

I believe most people never truly give themselves *permission* to write. Permission to write involves a number of critical elements. Permission means, as we've discussed, getting rid of the judge who whispers negativity in your mind and kills your will to write. Permission also involves **releasing** your passion. Permission feeds into passion, and passion fuels the words you select that define your 'writer's voice'. The more you allow yourself **permission** to write with *passion*, the more your positivity will feed on itself.

Passion: each of us has it for a topic, or even multiple topics. Passion is something that is best served raw. Let me explain. When you place raw passion on the page, there is no censor, there is no critic, there is no judge - it's just you, the page, and what roils within. Your passion doesn't have to be pretty. Your passion doesn't even have to be logical. What your passion **must** be, is released. Allow what you want to say to come out. After all, who is looking at your manuscript? (Hopefully no one but you at this point.) This is between you, the page, and your passion. Give yourself the freedom to get it all out. We'll clean it up later.

Fortitude comes next. Getting started is not the key ingredient, although without that first step, there is no book. Writing is about perseverance. Sitting down to write on days when you just don't feel it; keying your words consistently each day even though you have a thousand other things to do. Realizing that writing 1000 words will only take up about an hour of your time. Writing is a stick-with-it-no-matter-what endeavor. The funny thing is, on those days when you sit down and you just don't feel it, at least in *my* experience, some of your best writing comes out. By using the 'freewriting' method of simply writing your stream-of-consciousness, you may find yourself in a major breakthrough. You look up and you've written 3000 words. This happens to the people who persevere.

Finally - *forgiveness*. Writers must forgive themselves for various things. Things like missing a day. Things like not meeting a word count. Things like not writing perfect sentences. Things like not keeping their index cards with them at all times so that when a great idea presents itself, they can write it down immediately. This is **huge**. I cannot convey how many incredible ideas I've lost because I simply didn't write them down when I thought of them. The tragedy always plays out the same. I say to myself, "This is so good, I *know* I will remember it." Most often I don't, and the disappointment I then feel can be trouble to my writing. You *must* forgive yourself, and persevere. The word "perseverance" by definition means that there are obstacles. If the path was smooth, you wouldn't need perseverance.

Writing a book well begins with bestowing permission

on yourself to write passionately without judgment, just as your book lives inside you. Writing well will sustain the power of your passion and provide you with the fortitude to stick with it even though at times your enthusiasm may wane. And writing well must also contain an element of forgiveness for whatever mistake or blunder you may perceive you've committed. There is no right or wrong in writing. The only prerequisites you have are listed in this little 785 word package of encouragement. As long as you can commit to the two P's and the two F's - Permission, Passion, Fortitude, Forgiveness - you have what it takes to write.

Set your sights each day on these four words and you will successfully write your book.

Write your words today even if they have nothing to do with your book. Believe it or not, your book will benefit!

"Go Write and You Won't Go Wrong!"
~ Michael Ray King

Writing Tip #6

Daily Deadline

Sometimes, I'll send out the tips and encouragements late in the evening. Writers often put off writing for many reasons, most of which are simple distractions. One way to preserve your writing time is to make a point each day to set a writing deadline for yourself. I plan my writing time and set my deadlines the day before.

Let's say I have a particularly busy day scheduled for tomorrow. I may set a 10:00pm deadline by which to get my writing done. We tend to be more responsible to our deadlines than we are to ourselves. By meeting your deadline to write, you actually accomplish both.

Writing often brings about a euphoric feeling. Some of us (I surely do) use writing as a means of working out internal issues. Therefore, by meeting your writing 'deadline' each day, you not only move another major step forward on your book, you also take care of yourself – a win-win situation.

I recommend you take your writing seriously. Consider setting a deadline if needed. I have a failsafe deadline of 11pm. One other thing, if you know you're going to be out of town, plan when and where you will have Wi-Fi. Make sure you schedule time in your itinerary to write. I failed to plan for just such a situation once and missed writing three days in a row. So far this year, I have written all but seven days. I will not miss another. Make sure you keep the writing of your book at the top of your daily radar screen and look forward to it!

"Go Write and You Won't Go Wrong!"
~ Michael Ray King

Go Write and You Won't Go Wrong
Writing Tip #7

Affirmations All-Around

While writing my first book, my mentor noticed I'd get bogged down a bit. He had me print out sentences and phrases in very large fonts. Sentences and phrases like: "I am an author!" and "Michael Ray King - author of the book Fatherhood 101" and "I will finish my book." He then had me cut these sentences and phrases out and tape them to mirrors, the refrigerator, in the car on the dashboard, etc. Basically places I would see each day.

You are currently writing your book. Getting positive feedback from your book's number one fan – (you) is important. I even made a mock-up cover for my book and put it beside my computer monitor. You become your own cheerleading squad. Who better to lead the cheer? You know those "Chicken Soup" guys? They put posters all over their homes and offices - NEW YORK TIMES BEST SELLER. Look at them now!

Only *you* can write *your* book. Someone else may write on a similar topic, but no one else can write your words, your thoughts, your ideas. You have your own voice, developed out of your passion, experiences and goals. Writing is a solitary endeavor. Remember when I advised you to keep the inner workings of what you write to yourself during the creation stage? That's because maintaining the momentum is one of the toughest challenges for new writers. Cheer yourself on!

Reward yourself with some decadent dessert or a shopping spree or a day at the beach when you complete chapters. Cheer yourself on with positive statements posted around your house. Make a mock cover of your book and envision its completion. I'm telling you true, in the end, you will be glad you did!

"Go Write and You Won't Go Wrong!"
~ Michael Ray King

Writing Tip #8

Positive Proclivity

A few years ago I started up a 'focus' writers group. We call ourselves the Rogues Gallery Writers. Currently we have five members, but one is on an extended 'maternity leave'. She just had her third child and they are all about two years apart, so she's pretty busy.

The importance of my focus writing group for you is this: I learned, in a **huge** way, that watching others strive to accomplish the same thing I'm working on helped motivate me. The Rogues Gallery Writers wrote a novel together. We each wrote our own chapters. When one of the other three would send out an email with their chapter attached, I would get pumped myself!

All that said, in the course of this book/webinar, I'm going to send you a link to a Google Spreadsheet file. Each of you will be able to access the file. Basically, the file is similar to an Excel spreadsheet. Each of your names will be on the sheet. I would like you to post how many words you write each day, underneath your name. I'm also including a column for your index cards. I would like to see how many index cards you knock out each day.

Use this as encouragement. When you see someone else putting up numbers, allow that to spur you on. When you see someone post a zero, recognize that life stepped into their writing project just as it steps into yours and mine. Most anything can be looked at from both a positive and negative view. I am encouraging you to use this Google Spreadsheet for inspiration.

Sharing information like this with people who are not writing, is an exercise in disappointment. Non-writers do not understand the magnitude of your accomplishment. Sharing with others who are in the midst of the same task as you brings support and camaraderie and motivation. My encouragement for you today is to share your writing trek with those who will understand your challenge most.

Look for my invitation to share the Google Spreadsheet!

"Go Write and You Won't Go Wrong!"
~ Michael Ray King

Go Write and You Won't Go Wrong

Writing Tip #9

Perseverance

Perseverance. I won't know until we speak each week what obstacles you may be running up against. Possibly you're tooling along just fine. One of the goals I have with this program is to de-mystify the act of writing a book. Once you understand that the tenacious writer wins the day, you understand that only **you** have the power to stop your dream. Once you grasp the simplicity of writing each day, piecemeal, and to build the book over time by writing from a position of passion each day, you will wonder why you didn't do this year's ago. At least that was my experience.

I encourage each of you to persevere. I also encourage you to email me. I may not be able to get back to you right away, but I will get back to you. Use me during this webinar or class time. I'm learning as well. I desire to deliver this webinar on a much larger scale and I have already learned *major* things that will help me streamline the endeavor, thanks to your input. Stick with the process. It doesn't matter if you fall behind. Truthfully, there is no "behind". You write your book at your pace. I'm teaching you how to do it in 30 days. There is no law that says you must complete your book in 30 days.

If you persevere and you do what I say, you **will** have your first draft done in that time frame. The great thing about is YOU CAN DO IT! Keep that judge away. Kill the critic. Write. Everyday. Perseverance writes this book!

"Go Write and You Won't Go Wrong!"
~ Michael Ray King

Writing Tip #10

Time of Day

Thus far, the encouragements have travelled along these lines: eliminate the judge; find your writing zone; go past your 1000 word minimum when you're "feeling it"; remember permission, passion, fortitude and forgiveness; set a daily "writing deadline" the day before; post affirmations around the house; share your success with those on the same trek as you (use Google Spreadsheets if in my writing workshop); and persevere.

The time of day you choose to write can play a large role in your creativity. Scientifically it has been proven that just before going to sleep and just after waking up, our creative nature is at its strongest. You'll find *many* writers who will tell you writing early in the morning or late at night is their "special time." Just because these studies support this phenomenon, that doesn't mean quality writing doesn't happen other times.

Personally, I plan my writing time when I know I can be relaxed and "into" the writing. While this does not always work out the way I expect - life happens - at least I create the idea of looking forward to the relaxing time I'll spend writing. This tip is related to setting a writing deadline. The difference is, here, you're picking out what you feel is your *best* time of day. With the deadline, you're drawing a line in the sand that says, "If I haven't written by this time, I will sit down and write."

"Go Write and You Won't Go Wrong!"
~ Michael Ray King

Go Write and You Won't Go Wrong
Writing Tip #11

Commitment

4:00am! Whew! I'm off to West Palm Beach for a mini conference. I've knocked out my minimum words for the day, and now I'm making sure I'm taking care of my other writing commitments. I'm learning a number of things during this process. Here's the tip for the day from what strikes me at this early hour.

Like any endeavor worth pursuing, writing is a commitment. Just like your business or job. When you get pressed and don't feel like working, do you pack it in and say to yourself, "I just don't feel like it today?" Ok, I know, sometimes we do this, but hopefully not often. Anything worth pursuing requires commitment.

Little voices in your head will be prone to say, "hey, I'm not making money on this (yet)," or "the world won't end if I don't write today," or any number of similar statements. I consider the conscious choice **not** to write as a small step away from a dream. Yes, sometimes taking a rest is something a person must do. I recognize most people are not as driven to write as I am. There's nothing wrong with that. In fact, taking that break can be healthy.

But I also know the pitfalls of getting out of rhythm with what you desire to accomplish. Commitment will get you there. Sounds a bit like perseverance, and it is. But commitment is so much more. My experience with the desire to write a book is that keeping your heart invested in what you're doing brings joy and anticipation into the process, where perseverance keeps you moving forward.

So add a dash of "heart" to your perseverance recipe for success and commit to writing each day. On those days where your heart struggles, allow perseverance to take the helm, knowing your commitment remains within you. When you invest your heart and your effort in working toward a dream what happens?

You get there...

"Go Write and You Won't Go Wrong!"
~ Michael Ray King

Go Write and You Won't Go Wrong

Writing Tip #12

Expectation

When you think of writing every day, what's your first thought? *Writing today?* I certainly hope I can squeeze some time in. *Writing today?* Not a chance. *Writing today?* Why should I bother? No one will read it anyway. *Write today?* I don't feel like it. *Writing today?* As long as I get these other tasks done, I'll reward myself with a wonderful, luxurious hour of writing.

I could share dozens of other answers I've used over the years to the question. My "answers" aren't important, here.

I'd like to appeal to your sense of dedication and interest in getting your book written. I wake up each morning now with the **expectation** that I'll write. Nothing along the lines of "if" or "when I get done with" or any other derailment. I expect to write my minimum words every single day. This is a mindset I would love to inspire in each of you.

Even if you don't get your 1000 words written. Even if you don't get 750 words written. Even if you only write for 5 minutes and get 97 words written, I urge you to possess an expectation to write every single day. This relates to the other tips I've passed on like commitment and permission, and perseverance. Expectation is slightly different in that you develop a confidence and an energy *within you* that reflects permission, commitment, and perseverance. Taking those three items and *expecting* to write, you step into the realm of "writer".

Some writers take years and years to write their books. I understand. I took two years to write my first. I can in all certainty and honesty say, during those years, I did not give myself permission nor committed to write every day. I therefore did not persevere every day in my writing, and I certainly did not **expect** to write every day.

My encouragements are to inspire you to step into the responsibility of making your writing dream come true. I can do many things to help and inspire. The one thing I cannot do is write *your* book. So please, cultivate a climate within yourself of expectation. Each night before you go to bed, tell yourself of your expectation to write the next day. Wake up with that expectation. Follow through with that expectation. When you do these things, the positivity takes hold and you'll wonder why you didn't do this in the first place.

"Go Write and You Won't Go Wrong!"
~ Michael Ray King

Go Write and You Won't Go Wrong

Writing Tip #13

Resolve

Do you learn well from other people's stumbles? In 1979 a college professor suggested to me that I write for a living. I chose to deny my inner desire. I fought my way through retail management for 25 years. Then I almost died of peritonitis on an operating table in November 1999. I'd been saying to myself for twenty years, "someday I will be a published author."

I'm here to let you know that "some days" never happen unless you make them happen. When you truly find your desire, you must step up and go for it. Even though I vowed to pursue my dream of writing as I recovered from surgery, it still took me almost eight years to write my first book. Since 2008, I have written *eight* books. This week, I'm going to write another. Nothing changed but the resolve to make something happen.

Since I appear to be on a 'word-of-the-day' streak, I'm going for the word "resolve." A multitude of voices lie in wait for writers to stumble over. Have you heard them?

"I'm not good enough."

"I can't do this."

"I don't know what to write."

"I don't have time."

"What I've written is crap."

"Who'd want to read anything I have to say."

"I'll do it tomorrow."

What about that little (or large) critic? Has he/she popped into your head at any point yet? My bet would be yes, multiple times. The critic is the source of many of these negative internal voices. Keep that critic at bay!

There are literally thousands of other voices that will pop up into a writer's mind. Reasons not to write today abound. One of my favorites (from the past) is, "All these successful writers say to write every day, but I'm different. I know I can write, I'm just going to do it on my terms." That statement **does** hold *some* truth to it, but I must ask you to trust me on this. Writing every day is a major key to moving forward. Once I adopted daily writing, not only did I start seeing results, my writing improved.

Resolve to go after that book you've wanted to write. Do you know how many millions of people say they want to write a book as opposed to how many actually do? As long as your book is in your head as nothing more than a conversation piece, all you have is a dream. Once you write the book, you have a tangible, visible product that you created. Why I went from 1 book in 29 years (1979-2008), to 8 books in 4 years (2008-2012), stems in large part from the fact that I understand writing a book does not have to be a looming monster. Writing a book can be done quickly, efficiently and enjoyably.

Go Write and You Won't Go Wrong

You possess the power to accomplish the task of writing a book. You can learn this month what I spent three decades learning. I refuse to call that 29 year period a mistake. It simply was an extremely long lesson. Your lesson does not have to take that long. Trust me on this. You can write that book. You can do it in 30 days. Resolve to write every day and make it happen. Sitting back and thinking and wishing and resting on the word "someday" will not get you there. Resolve to get there and you will be amazed at yourself!

"Go Write and You Won't Go Wrong!"
~ Michael Ray King

Writing Tip #14

Writing Resources Handy

Here we go with another tip. One of the dynamics I've come to learn in writing is that everything happens for a reason. My first four-week webinar on how to write a book in 30 days got postponed the second week because I scheduled a flight the same time as the webinar. I would be over South Carolina when the live webinar was supposed to happen.

The plane flight that caused this two-day delay allowed me to put into motion some really cool new aspects I want to incorporate in future webinars. You benefit from some of the ideas that came from that mishap. Meticulous scheduling and planning are just two of the tasks to which I now pay close attention.

The same thing happens with your writing. One thing you'll find is that you keep getting these little ideas you want to incorporate into your book, often when you're out on a trip, at a meeting, at the grocery store, almost anywhere but in front of your computer. I encourage each of you to carry blank index cards with you to capture those ideas. I know though, that just because I suggest this doesn't mean you'll do it. So let me help make sure you don't lose these really cool ideas. The fact is, those ideas pop into your brain, but there's no guarantee they'll come back later.

Make sure you use **all** the resources around you. Have notepads and pen or pencil by your nightstand, in all your rooms, especially the kitchen and bathroom. That way, you have the tools to jot down a note. And do **not**

Go Write and You Won't Go Wrong

forget your everyday tools like your smart phone. You should have notepad capability on your phone. You may also have a voice recorder. Use them! Get those notes captured immediately so you don't lose them.

Some of the greatest stuff I've never written has been banished to an eternal death in the land of forgetfulness. To be fair, the issue is not forgetfulness, the issue stems more from our minds working overtime all the time and these little ideas get pushed out. Make sure you capture them. This is a critical part of the writing process. When you're writing on a project like a book, just because you walk away from your computer does **not** mean you aren't still writing your book - *you are*.

Your subconscious keeps at it even when you think you're done. Don't miss out on these wonderful opportunities to add more value to your writing. Capture those thoughts and ideas when they happen and go back and add them to your index cards later. I'm serious about the fact I've missed out on loads of great writing because I did not take the time to write down the ideas. Too many of them were, "That's so good I'll never forget it!" Guess what happened in almost *all* cases? I forgot.

Have a GREAT WRITING DAY!

"Go Write and You Won't Go Wrong!"
~ Michael Ray King

Writing Tip #15

Confidence

Today's encouragement is *confidence*. Confidence helps get you past those inner voices (yes, you may call them demons) that drag you down. Confidence carries a writer to the finish line. Be confident you have something to say. Be confident in the fact that what you say has merit. I'm one of the most critical people I know concerning my own writing, yet I remain confident in my ability to write, my right to write, and first and foremost, that my message is valuable.

You want to write this book for a reason. Somewhere inside you, that reason desires to move forward. Until you show your writing to the light of day, you'll never know what can become of it. I would never have told you, even three years ago, that I would be a five-time Royal Palm Literary Award winning author. It wasn't even the remotest of dreams for me. The reason for the surprise in respect to the awards is that I don't write for awards. I'm delighted to win them, but I write for myself. That requires a certain level of confidence.

To write is to expose yourself to the world, or so it feels. The truth is, someone **will** read your writing. Most writers, if they are truly honest, fear this exposure. Step into your writing with confidence. The message or story or help you offer will benefit others in ways you cannot predict. When those voices rag you about your word count, your story or message, your dedication, anything – clutch confidence close to your heart; tell the voices "Thank you for your input, now sit down and shut up," or some other command palatable to you.

Confidence in your message helps you to seize the day. You can write your book, I have every confidence in you!

"Go Write and You Won't Go Wrong!"
~ Michael Ray King

Writing Tip #16

Google Spreadsheet

Today's encouragement comes from my everyday writing life. I've heard this from others who write as well. Looking at the big picture of a project can be daunting once you've stepped into the task of achieving your goal. There are many views on how to handle this. The famous "How do you eat an elephant? One bite at a time." is the most prevalent view. Others, like Brian Tracy, say "eat that frog." which means address the toughest tasks first to allow yourself the view of everything else being simple. Others say to knock out the easy stuff, gain momentum then take on the big tasks.

Scientifically, to-do lists tend to be major landmines. People load up their day with 10 items on their list and typically complete three. The general thinking is to only put three things on your to-do list. Either way, you get three done, but one way you feel only 30% successful, the other you feel 100% successful. Personally, I've tried the 3-on-the-list method, but I really need to be accomplishing much more than three tasks in a day. If I plan to do three and I accomplish them, I feel like doing more as a bonus, not a burden. Since I don't want to forget all the tasks I need to do, I write them all down.

Here's a system that works for me and it might be of use to you, too. Mostly this is a "mindset" thing. I created a Google Doc Spreadsheet labeled "Mike's Daily Tasks". Across the top of the spreadsheet I have columns set for each day of the week, Monday through Sunday. In the next row under each Day of the week, I

Go Write and You Won't Go Wrong

have the exact date. I skip a line and begin listing tasks I need to do the next day, numbering them from "1" to however many tasks need to be done.

The next day, I begin knocking tasks out. Often I may do task #1 and #2, then skip to #6 or some other task out of sequence. Things happen during the course of one's day that may accelerate importance or diminish importance of a task. Many times I have to add a task I'd forgotten or one that came up during the day. I add this to the list because of what I do next....

Each time I complete a task, I go into the toolbar at the top of the spreadsheet and change the "Text Background Color" to light blue. This denotes completion of that task. Keep in mind Google Spreadsheets are 'cloud computing' meaning I can access this information from any computer or my smart phone. Therefore, I can be anywhere and complete tasks and mark them *done*. I'm writing this on a Thursday. So far this week, Monday I completed five of nine tasks. Tuesday, six of seven. Wednesday, five of seven.

When I get to the end of the day, those tasks not completed get moved to the next day and any new tasks get added. I use a different "Tab" (page) for each month, but since I run Monday-Sunday, the last few days of one month and the first few of another stay in one month.

One of the benefits of using the Daily Task List, other than seeing completion rates on your tasks, is being able to go back and look at when you accomplished something. And seeing your productivity in color before your eyes is empowering. You can adopt this spreadsheet-type system to the writing of your subtopic index cards. Make a plan the night before, regarding what subtopics you'll write the next day. Key them onto your spreadsheet. The next day you have a plan, and a goal. Let's say you write two of the four cards you selected the night before, but you really want to write one you didn't select. Simply add it to your list and write it. This is another way of tracking your progress.

Also, be diligent to make up new index cards for any new subtopics you come up with. Otherwise, like one writer mentioned, you're doing a lot of writing but not seeing your completed stack of index cards grow. You'll also need those subtopic cards when you lay out the cards on the table to look at the overall plan for your book.

I believe in using technology as a tool to help me complete tasks. My task completion rate has jumped dramatically once I developed the mindset that most people only accomplish 30% of a 10 item list and I'm knocking out 60 - 90%. That motivates me. Yes, I do have a bit of a competitive nature, and I do like to see myself achieving above the norm. Nothing wrong with that in my opinion. If this helps, adopt it into your routine.

I have 9 things on my to do list today. 1 - Write 1000 words (this encouragement tip is already at 850 words). 2 - Write to the aspiring writers in the webinar (two birds with one stone, right? - Hey, build in positive motivators for yourself, there are no rules, so make up your own!). 3 - Revise a publishing contract. 4 - Post a completed video to my YouTube channel. 5 - Write

2000 words on my book. 6 - Prepare for a teleconference call. 7 - Line out index cards for a workbook. 8 - Blog. 9 – Develop a financial spreadsheet for a potential client project. I fully intend to accomplish all 9. Realistically, I may only hit 6 or 7 of them. I'm good with that. Note I did not break down how many index cards I'll write today. I'll get in my 2000 words with each index card running an average of 500 words. I've been doing this so long, I know I'll probably write 4 or 5 of my cards. I suggest you break it down unless you automatically think like I do. Plus, writing down each card is *very* motivational as you get to color in multiple tasks on your Google spreadsheet.

You don't even have to do what I've described here as long as you give yourself credit for accomplishing goals each day. Find a system that works for you. Use mine. Use parts of mine. Make your own up. Whatever gets you into forward motion brings you another step (or bite) closer to your goal.

"Go Write and You Won't Go Wrong!"
~ Michael Ray King
(1098 words! Woo hoo! I get to check off two tasks!!!)

Writing Tip #17

Resist Temptation

Yesterday was quite a day for me. I wrote over 4000 words, knocked out three chapters of my new book, and generally felt today would be just as good. The time is now 10:30pm and these words you're reading come as the first words written today. How does a writer fall from over 4000 words to nearing the 750word.com midnight deadline with nary a word written?

Life. Life and the realization that I'd earned a few hours off. Life and the feeling I earned a few hours off that became a whole day. When you have a great day like I did yesterday, and you will, be ready for a bit of a letdown. Even if you still ride the euphoria of a good writing day, you should pick yourself up and write the next day.

Growing up, dessert always came after dinner. Why? Because the temptation becomes too great to eat too much dessert, not enough good food, and consequently not eat a proper, healthy meal. The same can be true with writing. Maybe you're the person who could stare down a half gallon of cherry cordial ice cream and only sample a small bowl. I've never been that person. Maybe now that the lactose gets to me, but back in the day, you can bet all that delicious sugar called to me.

Something inside me whispered this morning, "Write now Mike, then go out a have a ball!" I didn't listen. Now I'm up late, tired, wanting to go to bed and needing another 750 words just to hit my minimum word count for the day. I must thank all of you for these

Go Write and You Won't Go Wrong

words, because writing tips and encouragements to you helps me meet that word count minimum. I encourage you to resist the temptation to put off your writing when you know the likelihood is slim that you will actually sit down and key. Remember, this is Write a Book in 30 Days. I don't want to come across as an unsympathetic taskmaster, but to complete this task, you must write every day.

My encouragement for this day is to plead with you to not only resist the temptation to put off your writing for later, but to also pay the price when you do. I sorely want to head to bed at this very moment. I look at my task list for the day and realize I blew off an entire day. I will rebound and make up for this tomorrow, I'm sure.

The reason I'm being so blatantly honest about my day is that I desire to get across to you that these things happen to everyone, even writers who consistently write every day. According to 750words, this writing will be my 59th day in a row of achieving my word count. Many, many issues have popped up over the last 58 days that could easily have snuffed this streak.

Determination and pursuit of goals is a mindset. Whether your pursuit is to write a book or some other project goal, where you direct your focus will determine where and when your goals will be met. Resist the temptation to blow off a day and expect this urge after a particularly great day of writing. When you do succumb to the temptation, pick yourself up, pay the price, tough it out and keep your promise to write every day.

One side note - If you look through the 750word.com

site, you will notice they offer a monthly challenge. I've entered every month this year. June will be the third month that I complete the challenge. I encourage you to challenge yourself with this. Have a great writing day!

"Go Write and You Won't Go Wrong!"
~ Michael Ray King

Writing Tip #18

PMA

What a beautiful day! Coming off two days of very divergent writing success, I'm motivated. One thing to focus on anytime you sit to write is PMA. PMA is today's encouragement.

I used to employ PMA with my bowling teams back in the early 90's. We liked to be competitive and enjoy ourselves as well. In many ways, PMA resembles today's *affirmations*. PMA stands for Positive Mental Attitude. In the bowling leagues, I encouraged my teammates to always envision themselves bowling a strike the instant they stepped foot on the approach.

I never, ever bowl without this attitude in my mind. I step on the approach and I'm thoroughly convinced I will roll a strike. I've bowled like this for decades. After writing yesterday's encouragement, I realized I practice the same technique when I write. Every time I sit behind my keyboard (or pen), I know words will flow. I know I will write something of consequence. I know my time will be rewarded with a day that's productive.

Since I'm not on the pro bowler's tour, you may well assume I do not always bowl a strike. I do carry a 200 average, which means I often bowl strikes. The same is true of my writing. I don't always write a brilliant manifesto, or poem, or short story. But with all the repetition and practice, I write well.

Approaching your tasks at hand with an inner confidence that involves "knowing" you will succeed, sure contributes to your desire and motivation, your confidence, and your anticipation and excitement to get back at it. No goal worth reaching comes easy. Much of the time in our lives, our goals lay just out of our line of sight. We get stuck because we don't give our best effort.

You cannot give your best effort unless you expect the best outcome. When you bowl, expect a strike. When you write, use your PMA and expect your best. Often you'll surprise yourself with brilliance you didn't know you possess. I'm back on track now. One huge day. One not so huge day. Both contain value. I write with PMA!

"Go Write and You Won't Go Wrong!"
~ Michael Ray King

Go Write and You Won't Go Wrong

Writing Tip #19

Wealthiest Place on Earth

Today's encouragement comes from this quote: "...the wealthiest places in the world are not the gold mines of South America or the oil fields of Iraq or Iran. They're not the diamond mines of South Africa or the banks of the world. The wealthiest place on the planet is just down the road. It is the cemetery. There lie buried, companies that were never started, inventions that were never made, bestselling books that were never written and masterpieces that were never painted." ~ Dr. Myles Munroe.

We not only owe it to ourselves, we owe our inner struggles and power to those with whom we share this planet in our lifetime. To rob the world of our stories or knowledge is to give our wealth to the cemetery, and by definition, the least impactful of places. Never believe your trials and struggles have no meaning in this world.

Each of us has something we've overcome, something we've come to understand, or something with which we've struggled. Sharing our answers, insights, and knowledge helps others to not feel alone, to realize there is hope, and to find a way through their trial. Understanding that **you** possess this power and that your control it, you will then go out and help others.

One way in which you do this is to write the book you feel compelled to write. Each time you feel or say you don't have the time, ask yourself, "if not now, when?"

We're not guaranteed tomorrow. We always possess the moment "now" until it's taken. Use this moment now and release *your* riches to the world, rather than holding onto them for the wealthiest place on Earth.

"Go Write and You Won't Go Wrong!"
~ Michael Ray King

Go Write and You Won't Go Wrong

Writing Tip #20

Writer's Voice

Today I'm encouraging you to allow yourself your own unique "writer's voice". Every successful writer possesses their own style. Granted, aspects of each writer's style or voice are borrowed from those who have gone before, but there is usually a personal element that identifies a particular writer. I realize this may feel a bit abstract, but your writer's voice plays a vital role in your writing. I wish to encourage you to use your own voice, rather than to try and make the words you write sound like someone else.

Writing from the heart will go a long way to getting your story delivered to readers in a way that encourages them to read more. Yes, there are grammar rules and punctuation. Did you know some of the most famous writers of all time couldn't spell? Good editing cleans up a book, but without the writer establishing his or her voice, no amount of editing will propel a story forward.

Give yourself permission to be you**.** Allow *you* to flow over into your writing. Remember; keep The Critic under lock and key. Don't worry about the editing. A good editor will capitalize on your *voice* and help boost your writing to another level. I communicate with quite a number of people through blogging. I tell you true, there are a couple of writers who I can identify without even looking for their name. Their style and voice come through clearly. The key to this is simply allowing yourself to be *you*. That is what the reader desires anyway.

"Go Write and You Won't Go Wrong!"
~ Michael Ray King

Writing Tip #21

Digital Distractions

Today I've run into a very real and present danger to my writing mojo. These days I'm great with getting rid of the judge and critic. I schedule times and writing tasks each evening for the next day. I motivate from the positive progress I make as I check off each task item upon completion. I look to others who are writing and get motivated by their excitement, progress, and dedication.

But I discovered my greatest hurdle to writing these days is the Internet. I realize my malady is not uncommon. Yahoo news, crazy, goofy things that happen in this world caught on video, Facebook and its ability to suck me into my friends' and family's lives - all these things and more whittle away hours before I begin writing.

This situation of Internet distraction goes against the grain of my championing digital tools to help people write books. I now feel I must put a disclaimer on the recommendation to use Internet based tools. Don't get me wrong, I still back them 100%. I use them daily myself and they are effective. I simply need to warn you of the dangers of getting sucked in to the distraction-based Internet.

The insidious nature of this is that a lot of times, or in my case, most of the time, you feel like you are doing something productive. I answer emails, post something on Facebook (ok, not so productive...), I read up on things that will help me write. I keep abreast of the news and important happenings from local to worldwide importance.

However, none of that "surfing" is getting my book written. I look up and two hours have vanished. Writing requires discipline. For creative folks *discipline* is spelled *W-O-R-K* which is, quite obviously, a four letter word. I much prefer to write without a whip cracking over my head. I aspire to write from my heart and with honesty.

So instead of discipline to win the day over Internet distraction, I prefer the word "focus". I can focus on the importance of my writing. I can focus on the desire to get my book into the light of day. I can focus on writing being the single most important task of my day. For some reason, that focus works incredibly well for me.

Whatever it takes for you, if you run into IDS (Internet Distractions Syndrome), find a way to defend your writing from this consuming disease. Go analog (pen and paper) if need be, just flee IDS with every fiber of your heart, soul, and mind. Prioritize your writing. Set up a reward structure for completing your writing.

Hmmm. I see a decadent bowl of ice cream in my future....

"Go Write and You Won't Go Wrong!"
~ Michael Ray King

Writing Tip #22

Exercise Energy

Today's encouragement comes more from my coaching and personal experiences than it does with the actual writing of your book. I have found balancing my life brings rewards to my writing. By balancing my life, I'm talking about taking time out for exercise, interaction with family, interaction with friends, rest, and yes, work.

Today, I decided to take a walk before working. The exercise stimulated me and placed me in a better frame of mind to set about doing the tasks of the day. I like exercise early in the day because of the positive effects it has on the body and mind. Being ready to sit down and write reaps all kinds of good things for the reader. Also, while I walked, I thought of ideas I want to incorporate not only into my book, but into my day as well.

Typically, I prefer to take a bicycle ride, but since I'm in West Virginia at this writing, a walk sufficed. Your exercise should be voluntary and something you look forward to doing. When I'm in the midst of a writing project, physical exertion often leads to great ideas. Find that physical activity that gets you moving and helps you focus. Consider starting your day with exercise. See if the activity helps you with your writing project. I believe it will.

"Go Write and You Won't Go Wrong!"
~ Michael Ray King

Go Write and You Won't Go Wrong

Writing Tip #23

Trust Your Instincts

I received an email today about how one writer felt her writing was becoming more "textbook" writing than conversational. This made the writing dry and more difficult for her. This is a good time to remind you that your voice is the key in your first draft. Write your book as you *feel* it. Like this author did, when you feel your voice disappearing, allow yourself to step back into a "conversational" mode in your writing.

Remember, rewriting and editing will smooth away a whole lot of bumps. Getting your draft done should be about you and what you want to say. Keep it lively and interesting.

I'm taking the email mentioned above and making a writing tip out of the message. The writer titled the email, "Another Milestone or Breakthrough". Her recognition of her mindset and the adjustment she made is definitely useful in writing. When you feel yourself struggling with your words, there is a reason.

I'm not going to suggest you go back and analyze your writing as that will set The Critic free. We don't want to see The Critic. But you can trust your instincts. Keep your writing enjoyable. Keep yourself in a writing mood. Allow your voice to shine through in the writing and you will walk away eager to get back at it the next day. I'm suggesting you trust your gut; trust how you feel about your writing while doing it. If the writing begins to be a chore, find a way to get back to your *voice*.

Your inner *voice* wants to write this book. That's why you took on this endeavor. When that inner voice gets choked off, you are no longer in alignment with yourself and the writing becomes a struggle. When you allow that inner part of yourself to have its "say" in this world, you'll find yourself more prone to write.

I totally enjoy this kind of feedback from writers. These insights help others to achieve their goals just like I'm working to help each of you achieve your writing goals. The writing community happens to be a very "sharing" community. I've set up a Facebook Page for participants of this webinar. This is a lifetime invitation, meaning you will be able to converse with people who take the webinar in the future. Make sure you "Friend" me on Facebook. That way I can invite you to the page!

"Go Write and You Won't Go Wrong!"
~ Michael Ray King

Go Write and You Won't Go Wrong
Writing Tip #24

Change of Venue

I'm looking forward to flying to by home state this evening. Part of the reason for this comes from the fact that I feel comfortable in my hometown surroundings. I'm looking forward to writing in different venues. Places like the pool, restaurants, and the library call me as writing locations. I know I can do that here, but simply being in West Virginia affords me a *different* place to write.

There come times in writing where changing up your routine can boost your writing enthusiasm. I'm looking forward to finding a nice restaurant where I can go, have a nibble, and write to my heart's content.

Today's encouragement is for you to look at your writing "routine" if you have one. As long as the routine serves you well, keep it going. But if you feel your writing could use a "spruce up", a little change of scenery, I encourage you to give it a try. You may have to test a number of locations before you find one that fits your writing needs. Personally, I need a Wi-Fi location since much of my writing is Internet based.

I love the pool, though. I may sacrifice the Internet availability just for the opportunity to take a refreshing dip every half hour or so. Writing should get your respect and even your disciplined approach to making it happen, but that doesn't mean you can't enjoy the time spent writing. Some of the excellent side effects of changing up your location can be a purer, more conversational writing voice. Another could be more of an eagerness to get back to the writing. Combining places you love to be with your writing can positively influence not only your writing voice and your anticipation to write, the new rhythm may even help you get more balance into your life.

Give a change of venue a whirl unless you're in a good place. Have fun with it and pay attention to how you feel writing in different places. The *travelling* writer can be loads of fun!

"Go Write and You Won't Go Wrong!"
~ Michael Ray King

Go Write and You Won't Go Wrong

Writing Tip #25

Edit on the Fly

You've been writing for many days now, so I'm going to suggest a bit more progressive tip.

I spoke with Lisa today, one of my first webinar participants. We discussed how I like to make my rewrite and edit stages a bit easier by using the "ounce-of-prevention" technique. **WARNING: If you do this, you must maintain a tight leash on your inner critic and judge.**

Here's the tip - when I write my first drafts, I stay conscious of a number of "types" of words that take power away from my writing. When I spot them, I replace them right then and move on.

"To be" verbs. One of the primary red flag groups. For those who don't remember their elementary school English, "to be" verbs are: is, was, were, are, had, has, have, etc. These verbs show the reader nothing. . Often, when I'm tempted to write a "to be" verb, I search for a much stronger verb before moving forward.

If this slows your writing way down, do not use this tip. The important focus is to get your manuscript written. You can clean up "to be" verbs later. I discovered over the past thirteen years of writing, that the editing process is simpler if I don't end up staring at a mountain of "to be" verbs in my first draft. Another benefit to jacking up the "verb power" in the first draft comes from the fact I often think *deeper* and write with more power when I use stronger verbs.

Remember, I've trained myself to do this over the past decade. Pre-weeding out "to be" verbs does not slow my writing down much. You should pay close attention to what you write, how long the writing takes, and if you can still write with passion while using this tip, use it in the writing of your first draft. If not, go ahead and just write your book and you'll weed out the "to be" verbs in the editing phase.

-ly adverbs. I also target words that end in *-ly*. These words are adverbs. Adverbs, almost without exception, weaken the power of the verbs that follow them. The weakness may be difficult to see sometimes, but in almost every case of an adverb preceding a verb, the verb is weakened.

Words like, *that, it, just, seems, try*, etc ninety-nine times out of one hundred, should never see the light of day. Yesterday I read a manuscript where a "Sir Godfrey" pressed himself on a maiden when he trapped her in a garden. The story takes place in the year 1066AD. The author wrote, "Mary turned quickly to try to get away."

First, no one turns in order to "*try* to get away." The woman turned to "get away". Note the *-ly* word in this sentence. This particular adverb comes **after** the verb. This should tell the author they selected a weak verb. Better to write, "Mary whirled around and bolted for the gate." This tells the reader she was doing more than *trying* to get away. Mary did everything in her power to get away.

Go Write and You Won't Go Wrong

Please understand, all this can be handled in the rewrites and edits. I like to cut down on how much work I need to do after my first draft. Noticing these items has become second nature to me and by continuing to write, they will for you, too.

Remember! Both the critic and judge desire to slow down your writing and "get it right." If this tip slows you down or opens the door to your critic, jettison the tip and continue writing as you have been.

If you feel brave and want to exercise avoiding some of these words, go for it. You may find, as I have, that your writing level jumps up a notch or two on your first draft. I bring this up now because we stand just a few days away from the 30 day mark. Editing and rewriting come next, so a little practice now won't hurt, right?

You're doing great!

"Go Write and You Won't Go Wrong!"
~ Michael Ray King

Writing Tip #26

Divertive Ideas

When you write a book, many of the "hot topics" you desire to write pop into your brain throughout the day. When you make sure a pen and paper or computer or some other means of capturing your ideas is close at hand, you help insure your ideas do not disappear into the mists of forgotten thought.

What about this scenario? You sit down to write and you progress into your next subtopic. A quarter of the way through, a tremendous idea rocks your world. You know you must capture the idea. What do you do?

On one of the calls in the first webinar, we discussed this scenario:
Do you keep writing until you get to a stopping point?
Do you stop, write down the idea, then go back to writing?
Do you stop and proceed with the new idea until you flesh it out?

Of the first two suggestions, my recommendation is to stop what you are currently writing and jot down the gist of your idea. Make sure you capture enough to remember your inspiration. Now, this could present a minor problem if what you are currently writing at that moment is hot. If you're on fire, divert to your idea only a moment, then get back to your writing.

The third suggestion brings up something only you as the author can answer. If what you're writing at the moment the idea arrives is not super-inspired, turning to

Go Write and You Won't Go Wrong

the inspired idea and fleshing that idea out may serve you better. After all, inspired writing, that passionate, "I'm into it" type of writing, resonates with readers. The readers pick up on your inspiration and fly with it themselves.

Any time you can get a reader super engaged in your writing, I believe you have to go for it. Unfortunately, only you can make that call. You must decide whether what you started with comes across stronger than the idea you just came up with. You may run into this more and more as you write. I know I do.

Ultimately, you must also look at your focus. Does the new idea fit well with your book or does the new idea fit the description of a bright, shiny object that will deflect you from your goal? When deciding between the options, take into account your focus - the completion of your book on the topic you set out to write. Most of the time, I jot the idea down on a piece of paper and continue with what I'm writing, so that I can maintain focus.

Every once in a while though, I do divert to the new idea because it fits my book's focus, and the new idea is highly inspirational. One of the reasons writing can seem difficult stems from the fact that we must choose which path to take. Going into the experience organized and focused arms you with your absolute best chance to complete your task.

"Go Write and You Won't Go Wrong!"
~ Michael Ray King

Writing Tip #27

Inner Voice Naysayer

This morning I accomplished the tough task of starting a new routine - bicycling every morning from 6-8. Today I started at 7:15, ended at 9:15. I struggled to get out of bed. I fought the urge to try again tomorrow because my start time slipped so late. I fought the inner voice that asked, "Do you really want to do this?"

That voice knows me. That voice knows I tend to cave when I'm feeling tired. Then the voice prods me with, "You know you have a ton of work to do today."

Typically, all this adds up to the perfect storm and I trudge dutifully into my day without the music of my iPhone and the turning of my bike wheels. Typically I fight through the day with work-dominated priorities, and the activities that I love take the back seat of a stalled-life vehicle.

Today I did something different. I stepped up and forced myself to move forward. I gathered everything within me and took step after step after step. I sold myself into determination without motivation. Seems a bit much to have to take on to do something I love, doesn't it?

I believe many of us train ourselves to self-sacrifice at all turns before we "deserve" to reward ourselves with our desires. This happens to writers often. In fact, for those who state for years a book inside them craves to get out, I submit this scenario plays out daily.

Go Write and You Won't Go Wrong

Why rob yourself of your dream? Why deny yourself something you wholly desire? Like the meditative solitude I need from my bike ride, I truly desire to write. I now write every day. I intend to ride or get some other exercise every day. I look at neither as a chore. I am eager to accomplish both.

I knew this morning I wanted to be on that bike. I knew once I got going I wouldn't want the ride to end. The same goes for writing. You know you want this book. You know you want to get it written. You know once you start writing you won't want to stop.

Yet we allow other aspects of our lives to rob us of our simple desires. I want to be in shape and I want the positive endorphins released from exercise. Why deny myself these things? What possible downside is there to what I want out of riding my bike? Better physical health, less weight to carry around, and a positive attitude. Hmmm.

What about your writing? What do you wish to attain from it? Is the book intended to help others? Does writing help you feel better? Does the time spent creating a book lift your spirit in some manner? Why deny yourself those positive additions to your life? Consider that when we are in good physical, emotional and spiritual health, everyone in our lives also benefits!

My point is fairly obvious. When those excuses show up that will keep you from writing, put your head down and bull through them. You know the experience will lift you up. You know once you get started you will walk away feeling like you accomplished something. You know you have a plan that will work.

Step aside from the inner voice that thwarts your desires. Step away from the tendency to sabotage yourself, and step toward your goal - each day. I'm finding, with my iPhone, there is no excuse not to write. On my bike ride I wrote my blog for the day. I stopped at a park bench for about twenty minutes and I wrote a blog. I hopped back on my bike, motivated to the max.

Did you know you can access 750words.com from your iPhone? I once wrote and uploaded my words to the site while tooling around in a canoe in a lake at Salt Springs in Florida. I had to paddle out near the middle of the lake for a signal, but I got it done.

A person once told me, "reasons not to write are only excuses." I believe that. Sometimes we must force ourselves do what we desire to do, crazy as that sounds. Make an effort today. I know you'll feel better afterward.

"Go Write and You Won't Go Wrong!"
~ Michael Ray King

Go Write and You Won't Go Wrong

Writing Tip #28

Getting Ahead - Nanowrimo

Mark Twain once said, "The secret to getting ahead is getting started." This does not mean achieving your first ten thousand words. This means each and every day stepping into your destiny and writing. Once you complete your first draft manuscript, you then possess something of tangible value. Until you unlock your heart and allow your brain to spill words onto the page, you still lack that "getting started" of which Twain spoke.

I would like each of you to mark November 1st of **every** year on your calendar. November 1st begins the month of Nanowrimo which stands for "National Novel Writing Month." I have entered the Nanowrimo five times and completed the 50,000 words necessary to win three of those times. Interestingly, the two years I failed to reach 50,000 words (32,000 in 2008 and 37,000 in 2010) were each even numbered years.

In 2007, when I completed my first "novel in 30 days" with Nanowrimo, I learned firsthand what it takes to write a book in 30 days. My struggles each and every year taught me quite a bit about myself and about putting words into a manuscript. Each year, the key ingredient missing from my writing was a "structured" book. The three years I completed Nanowrimo, the books I completed left quite a bit lot to be desired.

For this reason, I put together the "Go Write and You Won't Go Wrong!" way to complete a book. Building your book structure up front with the index cards, allows you to come out on the other end with a manuscript worth editing. As much as you may look at your current manuscript and realize the edits will be many, my three Nanowrimo books require **massive** help.

Consider entering the Nanowrimo. You will find huge support from all around the world. Thousands upon thousands upon thousands of folks enter the Nanowrimo. Entry is free, by the way. People meet in cities and towns across the nation to support each other in their novel writing. You don't have to write a novel either. Your book can be nonfiction.

Take a page out of Mark Twain's book by following his advice. The secret to getting ahead is getting started. Plan on ways to keep your writing dreams alive. All the time.

"Go Write and You Won't Go Wrong!"
~ Michael Ray King

Writing Tip #29

Efficiency and Fun!

Focus on one - have some fun - git r done! This mantra has become one of my mainstay internal mechanisms for making things happen in my writing. I noticed some time ago that the fun had slowly dwindled from my writing like a balloon losing its air pressure in a dark corner of the room.

A call to my sister, who is an accountability partner with me, brought the "have some fun and just get it done" part of that internal chant. I added the "focus on one" part because I get distracted by 'shiny objects.'

You know what I'm talking about. Writing projects and story lines and articles and blogs and all these other writing related tasks that look like so much fun steals the time and energy from my books. So staying focused on a book becomes a challenge at times.

There are other distractions as well. Chores, bills, children, work, and a myriad of interventions conspire to wrench me away from completing the book. Even though the book is very important to me, the short term nature of these other things can sap the life out of the writing.

I give this to you as a mantra to chant when you start your day. The great thing is, this works for every single thing you wish to accomplish in your day. In fact, you may find that not only do you become more efficient in your day as far as accomplishing tasks you may also find you have a lot of fun.

Focus on one - have some fun - git r done.

Whatever you do, find a way to make that middle section, "have some fun", into a reality. Your days will be more enjoyable if you do!

"Go Write and You Won't Go Wrong!"
~ Michael Ray King

Writing Tip #30

Move Forward With Intention

When you're writing a book, staying with the writing can be the most difficult aspect of the entire process. You will be tempted to walk away. The crazy thing is, sometimes you need to take a break. In my last class we spoke of this a number of times. The important thing in this case is to not walk away from writing totally, but simply walk away from writing your book.

Continue to write your blog or a diary entry or an article or a free-write. Any writing will do, even if it is simply writing for the sake of writing. The idea is to defend your writing time. Make writing something you reward yourself with each day.

Your book will progress much faster if you do. I also should come more easily to you as you become accustomed to writing every day. The Critic must stay away until you finish your draft. Writing a book is almost as much about perseverance (as I mentioned in an earlier encouragement) as it is the writing itself.

Once you get that manuscript done, step away from it for a week or two. Line up four to eight people who will proofread your book and mark EVERYTHING they see. Use their input to strengthen the manuscript, then find and editor to put the finishing touches on it.

You can do this. Stick with it. Don't stop. Don't let The Critic sway you. Keep going and you will get your prize – your very own book!

"Go Write and You Won't Go Wrong!"

~ Michael Ray King
About the Author

Michael Ray King (1958 -) was born in West Virginia. He graduated from West Virginia State University in May, 1981.

His first book, *Fatherhood 101: Bonding Tips for Building Loving Relationships* won Honorable Mention in the Royal Palms Literary Award Contest in 2008. Michael is a five-time Royal Palm Literary Award winner. Three awards for Published Poetry, one for Unpublished Short Fiction, and an Honorable Mention for Educational Published Book.

Mr. King's writings cover topics such as poetry, writing, publishing, parenting, short fiction, and novels. His latest novel, *The Method Writers* was released in August 2012.

Go Write and You Won't Go Wrong: Write Your Book in 30 Days! is Michael's ninth book. His other eight books are available at Amazon, BarnesandNoble.com, and BooksAMillion.com. Their titles are:

Fatherhood 101: Bonding Tips for Building Loving Relationships
Loves Lost and Found
Writing is Easy
More Writing is Easy
Poetry in Black and White
Rock Your Business! Your Book as Your Business Card
Fictitious Fiction
The Method Writers

www.ingramcontent.com/pod-product-compliance
Lightning Source LLC
LaVergne TN
LVHW051845080426
835512LV00018B/3080